THE REAL PEAKY BLINDERS

BILLY KIMBER, THE BIRMINGHAM GANG AND THE RACECOURSE WARS OF THE 1920s

CARL CHINN

LARGE
PRINT

First published in Great Britain 2014
by
Brewin Books Ltd.

First Isis Edition
published 2015
by arrangement with
Brewin Books Ltd.

A catalogue record for this book is available
from the British Library.

ISBN 978–1–78541–121–2 (hb)
ISBN 978–1–78541–127–4 (pb)

Contents

Introduction

With its captivating cinematography, charismatic performances, and dramatic title, the *Peaky Blinders* series on BBC2 seized the attention of viewers and critics alike in the autumn of 2013. Stylish yet dark, it was set in the back streets of Birmingham after the First World War and told of the rise to power of Tommy Shelby and his criminal gang of peaky blinders. Fashionably dressed, they were named after the weapon they used in fights: the peaks of their flat caps into which had been sewn safety razors and which were slashed across the foreheads of their opponents, causing blood to pour down into their eyes and blind them.

A veteran from the First World War whose mind was wracked by the horrors he had witnessed as much as it was fixated upon making as much money as he could unlawfully, Tommy Shelby was an absorbing character. He controlled illegal speakeasy type betting shops in and around Small Heath but now wanted to grab some of the rich and easy pickings from the protection rackets on the racecourses of England. These were run by Billy Kimber, the clever London gangster who controlled a brutal gang and who had become immensely wealthy from threatening bookmakers and providing them with expensive "services".

References to Birmingham pubs such as the "Garrison" and firms like the BSA evoked a powerful sense of place amidst a fast-moving, thrilling plot with a moody atmosphere that appealed to a national audience. Acclaimed critically, *Peaky Blinders* won two awards at the 2014 BAFTA Television Craft Awards and was a success for its creator, Steven Knight.

A Brummie himself, he explained to the *Birmingham Mail* on August 20, 2013 that he wanted to tell a story based on "family legend and historical fact. It is a fiction woven into a factual landscape which is breathtakingly dramatic and cinematic, but which for very English reasons has been consigned to historical text books". This exciting approach has led Roger Shannon, Professor of Film and Television, to praise the series as "an epic about the working class in Birmingham. It mythologises what life was like."

Yet the real stories behind the fictional characters of the *Peaky Blinders* are as dramatic, bloody and compelling as the mythologised epic. Tommy Shelby's arch enemy Billy Kimber is based upon a historical person; but this most powerful gangster in England was not a Londoner as shown in the series, he was a Brummie from Summer Lane. A forceful man physically, he was a feared fighter whose astute mind and magnetic personality drew to his leadership a loose collection of dangerous and ruthless men from Birmingham who dominated the highly profitable protection rackets on the racecourses of England.

Like Kimber himself, the members of this Birmingham Gang emerged from the disreputable gangs of pickpockets and thieves from the city who had terrorised racegoers before 1914. Collectively known as the Brummagem Boys, their origins lay in the 1870s, the decade in which the infamous slogging gangs of Birmingham emerged. From the early 1890s, this term for the city's hooligan gangs was interchangeable with that of peaky blinders, a name that quickly gained notoriety nationally and which has become part of working-class folklore in the city.

It is likely that many of the Birmingham Gang had once been sloggers or peaky blinders but its supremacy on the highly profitable racecourses of the south of England especially arose not only from their own viciousness but also from Kimber's shrewd alliances with the formidable McDonald brothers of the Elephant Boys of South London and George "Brummy" Sage's Camden Town mob. Their ill-gotten gains aroused the envy of the Sabini Gang of London and their allies who fought violently to oust Kimber and his men and take over their rackets. Unwilling to be pushed out, the Birmingham Gang and its confederates battled back fiercely in the blood-stained racecourse wars of the 1920s. Reviled by the press, this Birmingham Gang led by Billy Kimber were the Real Peaky Blinders and this is their story.

CHAPTER
ONE

Slogging Gangs and
Peaky Blinders

The attack on George Eastwood by a gang late on Saturday March 23, 1890 was so vicious that two days later the *Birmingham Daily Post* condemned it as a "Murderous Assault". Living in a back house in Arthur Street, that fateful evening George had gone for a drink in the Rainbow in Adderley Street. It was his misfortune that Thomas Mucklow was also there with his bully mates. A teetotaller, young George had ordered a ginger beer. That inoffensive act was mocked by the gang. They chaffed him for his principles and in a later report in the *Post* on May 29 it was stated that Mucklow said, "What do you drink that tack for?" He was told to mind his own business whereupon he challenged Eastwood to a fight, which was declined.

The gang left the pub a little before eleven o'clock, when Eastwood began to make his way home down Adderley Street. He had only gone a few yards, and was just under the blue-brick railway arches which went across the street, when Mucklow struck his innocent victim a violent blow. George fell down and "it is supposed that his head struck the kerbstone, with the result that his skull was fractured". Whilst he was on the ground, he was kicked and hit with the buckle of a belt by one of Mucklow's cowardly friends. Somehow George managed to get to his feet and, chased by the gang, he ran to his left, down Lower Trinity Street.

He must have been in fear of his life, but with the strength of someone fighting to survive he clambered up the wall of Allcock Street School and crossed the playground into Allcock Street itself. Desperate for safety, George must have banged on the door of the house of a Mr Turner who kindly gave refuge to the unfortunate man despite the threats of Mucklow and his bunch of ruffians who were shouting outside.

Later that night George Eastwood was taken in a dangerous condition to the Queen's Hospital in Bath Row. In addition to "serious bodily contusions, his head was fractured and his scalp cut in two or three places". The injury to his head was so bad that it necessitated the operation of trepanning — the drilling of a hole into his head and George had to spend over three weeks in hospital before he was allowed home.

Aged 26, Thomas Mucklow was the only one of the gang who was identified and arrested by the police. A carter, he lived in Adderley Street itself. Although he called upon good character witnesses, he was found guilty of unlawfully and maliciously causing grievous bodily harm. He was sentenced to nine months' hard labour in Birmingham Prison after the prosecution had declared that Mucklow had struck without provocation and had encouraged the others in the gang to beat their victim.

Almost two weeks after the dastardly attack on George Eastwood, it was brought to the notice of the readers of the *London Daily News*. On April 9, it highlighted a letter by a Birmingham inhabitant to a local newspaper. This person stated that the murderous assault had been committed by members of the Small Heath "Peaky Blinders". The letter also appeared in other newspapers like the *Edinburgh Evening News* and *Aberdeen Journal*. It seems to be the first mention of the peaky blinders, the name that would be given to the hooligans belonging to various gangs connected to certain streets and areas in 1890s Birmingham — gangs which were feared for their violence and fighting with metal-tipped boots, stones, belt buckles and sometimes knives.

Before this, hooligans in Birmingham had been called sloggers and they belonged to slogging gangs, a term that had arisen sixteen years before the attack on George Eastwood. On June 20, 1874, the *Leeds Mercury* reported sardonically that a delightful pastime called "slogging" prevailed in Birmingham. It explained that "this amusement is of the most exciting description and any number of people may enjoy it at no greater cost than the chance of a broken head". The parties engaged form themselves into opposing bands, which chase each other about and "throw large stones at each other as fast as they can". They give variety to their proceedings by throwing stones at inoffensive passersby, often women and children, whom they also assault and rob. It was stated that the police were nowhere to

3

be seen when these attacks took place and that most of those involved were mere lads.

This phenomenon of slogging had first come to notice two years before. On April 8, 1872, the *Birmingham Daily Post* drew attention to a riot by the "Slogging Gang". The day before was a Sunday and "a large body of roughs" had gathered in the neighbourhood of Cheapside to the "great consternation of the inhabitants". Numbering 400 strong, they termed themselves the slogging gang. After creating a great disturbance and smashing several windows, the gang had moved up towards the Hill Street area where "they threw brick bats and stones at the windows of the hucksters (general stores) and confectioners' that were open".

The shopkeepers had to put up their shutters to protect their premises, whilst one of them was hit by a brick and had to be taken to hospital. For some time the rioters terrorised the passers-by whom they stopped and insulted. Finally they took to their heels when approached by a small body of police. Running back towards Cheapside, the sloggers were dispersed by another detachment of the police.

It was apparent that slogging had not emerged suddenly and that there was not one slogging gang, as made clear when the *Post* noted that a number of teenaged boys had been charged with throwing stones and disorderly behaviour in Rea Street South on the night of April 9. Superintendent Spear told the magistrates that for the last three or four weeks there had been great complaints from the residents in and around Cheapside and Barford Street regarding the large numbers of boys who had gathered to break windows.

Each of the prisoners was fined 20 shillings — a week's wages for a skilled worker — with the option of three weeks' imprisonment. One of the magistrates hoped that the police would make special efforts to apprehend some of the offenders who were older than those who had been fetched before the court.

That next night, April 10, between 70 and 80 sloggers were seen across the town in Northwood Street and Constitution Hill. Armed with sticks and well supplied with large stones, some of them had stoned a police constable and then run into Cox Street. Two of them were arrested. John Gibbon was an engine driver aged thirteen who lived in Water Street, near to the disturbance. Not far away was Hospital Street, the home of Michael Lowry, a filer aged fourteen. Both were sentenced to fourteen days' imprisonment.

Two teenagers from the Sunday riot appeared at the same Police Court. William Cockerill was sixteen and a labourer and James Davies was fourteen and also a filer. Both were of no fixed abode. Charged with throwing stones and stealing herrings from the Market Hall, Cockerill was sent to jail for six weeks and Davies for three.

One of the four magistrates before whom they appeared was Dr Melson, who had suffered from the sloggers on the Sunday when some had gathered outside his house. In the absence of assistance he had gone outside and thrashed one of them with an ash stick. Dr Melson's son then followed the gang and grabbed hold of their leader. Because of this, the young man had been set upon and he returned home with his lip and ears cut and almost covered in blood.

Dr Melson pronounced that "this stone throwing nuisance was becoming perfectly intolerable, and the dangerous state of the streets of the town was fast becoming a proverb". He had complained about the nuisance until he was tired, "and he was determined that when any of these boys were brought before him, whether they had actually been seen to throw stones or not, he should deal severely with them".

Unhappily stone throwing continued to be a major problem and on March 30, 1873, the police were faced with serious outbreaks of violence in several locations. In Rea Street South officers were stoned by a mob trying to free a prisoner. Over in Farm Street, Hockley, passengers on an omnibus were pelted with mud and insulted and in Great Hampton Street both police and passengers on another omnibus were bombarded with stones and mud.

It was now clear that slogging gangs were increasingly associated with certain streets that had a reputation for their tough youths; and that as well as attacking the police and innocent bystanders these organised gangs were fighting each other. On March 29, 1873, the *Post* noted that there was a feud between the Bradford Street and Park Street gangs. Eighteen months later, Thomas Joyce was named as the captain of the Allison Street slogging gang and in late

September 1874 he and an Andrew Toy brought a charge of violent assault against a William Smallwood.

It was alleged that Smallwood was one of a gang of 20 men who had attacked Joyce and Toy on Deritend Bridge. He had used a strap with a buckle attached and caused severe damage to the heads of the two men. However an independent witness stated that Joyce and Toy had gone for Smallwood with knives and that he had defended himself with a belt. Smallwood was discharged as the magistrates asserted that he had given the complainants a good thrashing in self-defence.

Other slogging gangs included those from Milk Street, Barn Street, Benacre Street, and Sheep Street. They were also located in the central parts of Birmingham in Digbeth, Deritend, Gosta Green and Highgate. The first outbreak of slogging associated with these areas died down in the later 1870s, but when gang violence broke out again in the mid-1880s it had spread from the older parts of the city.

Prominent amongst the new sloggers were those of Aston: the Wainwright Street Gang; the Whitehouse Street Gang, which included the feared Simpson brothers; and the Ten Arches Gang, which lasted in one form or another for over 30 years. These smaller groupings could come together as the Aston Sloggers to fight the Nechells Sloggers as on August 15, 1886, when hundreds of men and youths had fought a pitched battle in and around Rocky Lane. Armed with heavy belts, sticks, brick ends and other weapons, they had caused such a disturbance that according to the *Birmingham Daily Post*, they had forced out the whole of the available police in Aston, whilst the Birmingham police near the borough boundary had to be augmented.

The terms sloggers and slogging gangs continued to be used throughout the 1890s, but was now interchangeable with the new name of peaky blinders. For example, on June 27, 1895, the *Manchester Evening News* carried the headline "Birmingham slogging gangs" relating to a short notice on the imprisonment of two men "for maltreating a third with a loaded life preserver and fire irons". All three were said to be "members of rival gangs of 'peaky blinders' who stand upon street corners, to assault passers-by, or get up fights with other gangs".

Yet it is the name of the peaky blinders and not that of the sloggers which gained more widespread attention — so much so that they were classed alongside other infamous gangs like the hooligans of London, the scuttlers of Manchester and the high rip of Liverpool. And it is the name of the peaky blinders and not that of the sloggers that has remained infamous and which has passed into folklore.

This is despite the fact that "the reign of the peaky blinders" was short-lived. Strong policing, heavy sentences and various social factors such as the influence of schooling and the growth of boxing clubs led to their disappearance in the early twentieth century. Indeed in June 1902, the *Sheffield Evening Telegraph* featured a leading article on hooliganism in London and stated that the peaky blinders of Birmingham had been suppressed. Yet if they had disappeared before the First World War and did not exist in the 1920s, the ill-fame of the peaky blinders and their lurid name infused as it was with violence and gangsterism ensured that they would not be forgotten. Moreover their unsavoury reputation was embellished by stories such as that which claimed falsely that they sewed razor blades into the peak of their caps which were then used as weapons.

Nothing of the kind is mentioned in any contemporary newspaper reports of the peaky blinders or sloggers. Indeed this tale seems to have arisen not from fact but from fiction — from John Douglas's novel, *A Walk Down Summer Lane*, which was set in the inter-war years. When it was published in 1977 it caused a furore as it was seen by many Summer Laners as both playing upon and reinforcing negative stereotypes of the area. Serialised in the Birmingham *Evening Mail* it was disliked by many folk who were angered that it seemed to portray The Lane as a place of squalor, drunken rows, and rough people.

In response, Pauline and Bernard Mannion wrote a more straightforward and realistic book called *The Summer Lane and Newtown of the Years between the Wars 1918-1938*. Pauline recognised that "lots of tales have been told about Summer Lane, some true, some fanciful", but stressed that she and her brother were genuine Summer Laners "who want their memories of life in the Lane in the 1920s and 1930s to go on record for all to read about".

The down-to-earth approach of the Mannions emphasised the neighbourliness of the people of

9

Summer Lane and their pride in their street — qualities which they shared with all those who lived in the poorer working-class neighbourhoods of urban Britain. They accepted that there were fights, especially on a Saturday night, but so too were there fights in many districts of England. Yet the Mannions made no mention at all of peaky blinders. That is not surprising as there were no peaky blinders in Birmingham in the 1920s.

Of course, just as with any big city, there were plenty of hard men in poorer working-class neighbourhoods. Notable amongst them in Summer Lane were the Kirbys. Their notoriety spread far and on March 21, 1927 the *Evening Telegraph* in Angus, Scotland included a short notice explaining that "Birmingham police are making a determined effort to cleanse the city of the gangs of hooligans, who, during the last five weeks, have been emulating the 'Brummagem Tykes' of thirty-years ago". In particular James Kirby aged 26 and Frederick Kirby 24, both of Tower Street, were each imprisoned for two months for a brutal assault on a policeman.

My Great Uncle George Wood was another hard man who would go on to become a sergeant in the 2nd battalion SAS in the Second World War. Born in 1915, he was my mom's uncle and grew up in Whitehouse Street, Aston. He told me that:

> we used to fight as kids with other streets. Avenue Road, Chester Street, Holland Road, Rocky Lane. Oh, we was cock o' the f— north, Whitehouse Street. There was me, Dougie Ayres, Jackie Hunt, Herbert

Mortiboy, Bobby Steel and another lot. People used to watch us fight. Fists. Knew you worn't hurting each other. Once you was on your arse you was out the fight. Never seen any kicking. If you was fighting then, you fought with a ring round you, copper'd only muck in if there was somebody getting hurt.

When he was older Our Georgie fought several tough nuts and won. One of them was Tiny M "and he was supposed to be the worst bloke in Aston. I fought him and stopped all the trams on the top of Whitehouse Street on the main road. Oh, I did belt him and chase him, couldn't catch him". Uncle George also knew the Kirbys well from the sixpenny hop dance at the Memorial Hall in Whitehouse Street.

They was good kids, the Kirbys was. There was a crowd on 'em. Bert, he was the flyweight champion of Great Britain. Jack'd fight Bert Taylor at Woodcock Street Baths and they'd be at another baths next week. That was the Bert Kirby down Whitehouse Street dance. They used to get a bottle and whiz it right up the middle of the dance floor while they was dancing. They'd get open the doors. The Kirbys used to be up the top. They used to come from different areas.

Our fight night was Friday night in Whitehouse Street. All the chairs in the dance used to be all around the side and when it first opened they used to start fighting with the chairs. Real cowboy do, over your f— head and everything, and then they used to

11

nail 'em all together to stop 'em. So they used to sit down and wait till the dance started and put their legs lying out and bump it used to go orf. We used to have a go then, I mean if you had a bird and you went up in the air over the feet.

Uncle George also recalled that "it's funny, different areas used to have different hats. Checked hat gang, brown hat gang" — but he never mentioned razor blades sewn into their peaks. By contrast in his fictional account of Summer Lane in that period, John Douglas wrote that some men wore a peaky blinder. He stated that the peak of the cap "was usually slit open and pennies or razor-blades or pieces of slate inserted and stitched up again".

In a fight, these caps were "whipped off the head and swiped across the opponent's eyes, momentarily blinding them, or slashing the cheeks". There is no evidence of caps being used in this way as weapons. Indeed any fighting man would have dismissed it as most unlikely. A flat cap is soft behind the peak. It would be difficult to gain any force or direction by "whipping it off the head" to deliver an effective swipe.

Another fiction is that the peaky blinders head-butted opponents with the razor-blade filled peak of the cap. Yet again there is no evidence at all for this and it is another highly unrealistic scenario — given the difficulty of getting enough power "to drop the nut" with a narrow peak rather than a forehead.

The story of razor blades sewn inside the peaks of caps is just that — a story. Cut-throat razors were used to slash with in fights but they were much too big to be sewn into a peak and were held by the handle. Safety or guard razors were smaller, but they were an American invention and did not begin to be advertised and sold in Britain until the mid-1890s. And they were expensive. In January 1896, the *Sheffield Daily Telegraph* advertised seven Sheffield hollow found razors of best steel with black handles and a roan leather case for twelve shillings and sixpence (62½ pence). This was over half the weekly wage of an unskilled labourer.

Safety razors were a luxury item, as was emphasised by the gifts for a fashionable wedding listed in the *Northampton Mercury* on January 20, 1899. It included a variety of silverware for the groom and also a set of safety razors. Moreover such razors were not disposable. Their edges still needed to be stropped and honed. Cheaper disposable blades for safety razors did not appear until the inter-war years. Until then working-class men shaved with cut-throat razors of their own or went to a barber's for a shave as they could not afford safety razor blades.

If razor blades were not sewn into the peaks of flat caps how then did the peaky blinders fight? An account in the *Post* of October 30, 1895 provides bloody details. The previous evening, two police constables were called to turn out a gang of between 20 and 30 peaky blinders from the Stag and Pheasant on the corner of Bromsgrove Street and Pershore Street. Once outside they caused another disturbance and one of them called Warner assaulted the policemen, who took hold of him to take him into custody. Thereupon the gang "commenced to kick and beat them". James Cuson aged 28 then kicked Police Constable Bennett in the stomach and released Warner. The two men were later arrested. Warner was sentenced to six months in prison and Cuson to six weeks with hard labour. He had been convicted eighteen times before.

Three years later Constable Bennett admonished a party of youths who had been ejected from a theatre for their disorderly conduct. According to the *Cheltenham Chronicle* of Saturday January 12, 1901, a peaky blinder called Thomas Walters took out a long pocket knife and plunged the blade into the officer's back. The wound was very dangerous "and must have been instantly fatal if the blow had fallen an inch lower". A youth though he was, Walters was sentenced to five years' penal servitude for malicious wounding. The Recorder regretted that he was unable to punish the prisoner more severely.

Amongst other weapons of choice for peaky blinders and sloggers were life preservers — a short, weighted club like a small truncheon or cosh. On Thursday June 27, 1895, the *Manchester Evening News* carried the headline "Birmingham Slogging Gangs". It reported that two members of a peaky blinder gang had been imprisoned for maltreating a rival gang member with loaded life preservers and fire irons.

One of the most notorious peaky blinders was Henry Lightfoot. Aged eighteen and a nail caster, on November 2, 1888 the *Birmingham Daily Post* reported that he, John Moore and Richard Chamberlain were "hardened criminals" charged with stealing eight brass door knobs. The characters of Lightfoot and Moore were declared to be "about as bad as they could be" and each was given nine months' hard labour. Since 1886, Lightfoot had been convicted four times for theft — including that of three pigeons, a duck, and a woollen jacket. Despite his imprisonment he went on to re-offend.

In August 1891 he gave his address as Greet when he was accused with three others of wilful damage to a hay rick in Acocks Green; in March 1892 he was supposedly a caster living in Bolton Road, Small Heath and was charged with stealing a football; and eighteen months later, he was now a painter when he and two others were brought before the magistrates for assault. One man held the victim down whilst Lightfoot and another kicked him. It was stated that they were well known in the district and that the three of them had previously been convicted of assault together. Lightfoot was sentenced to a month's hard labour.

Then on December 3, 1895, Lightfoot was one of the first men to be actually called a peaky blinder. Of no fixed abode, he was accused of being drunk and disorderly and of several assaults. Late on the previous Saturday night "he had imagined that he had a grievance against several men" in a beer house. He had dashed in and assaulted several people with a stick. He did the same to the landlord and his wife, and then marched up Hurst Street and Bromsgrove Street hitting everyone that he met.

Fearful of Lightfoot, people turned away from him. He then came upon Detective Tingle. Lightfoot "lifted the stick above his head and discharged a blow which beat down Tingle's guard and struck his head". Tingle managed to hit his assailant and knock him into the horseway but was pushed over by a companion of Lightfoot, who struck the officer again. After some difficulty he was taken to the police station.

In court Sergeant Richards said that Lightfoot "had many times been sent to gaol for assaults on the police, and was dealt with severely at assizes for an assault on the Hay Mills police". In response the Bench pronounced that he was "evidently a 'peaky blinder' of a dangerous type and would be sent to gaol for six months". The incorrigible Lightfoot continued to offend. Over the next twelve years he was jailed on five separate occasions for theft, burglary, and assault, whilst several times he was found guilty of gambling, drunkenness, gaming, using obscene language, and assault. His last conviction that is available was for the theft of twelve scrubbing brushes in 1907. He was now 33 and a moulder.

In reality, peaky blinders like Lightfoot took their name from the peaks of the flat caps that they wore. This was made plain in the Angus newspaper the *Evening Telegraph* on Thursday July 31, 1919. In a major article on "How epidemics of crime are caused", the author stated that "the hooligans of Hoxton and the 'Peaky Blinders' of Birmingham — so called because they wear peaked caps — are lively examples of imitative crime".

Flat caps with stiff peaks became popular with working-class men and teenaged boys from the later 1880s. Before then the "billycock", a type of bowler hat, was the preferred form of headgear, as was made plain in the *Post* on Tuesday May 19, 1891. An older man was found dead in the canal at Saltley. It was explained that he "evidently belonged to the working-classes" as he wore a dark blue serge suit, cord trousers, lace-up boots, and billycock hat.

By then, though, the billycock was rapidly dropping out of favour with younger working-class men and thereafter it is mentioned rarely in the *Post*. The fashion for flat caps with peaks was quickly adopted by the members of street gangs in Birmingham and led to the name of the peaky blinders. This derivation of the name is reinforced by the terms "peakies" or "peaky type" that was occasionally used for ruffians in Birmingham, as it was in the *Post* on Thursday January 18, 1900. One such peaky on my paternal side was my great grandfather, Edward Derrick.

Born in 1879, he was a thief, a violent man and a most reprehensible character. Nicknamed "Bummie", he led a life of crime like his grandfather, James. He had been born in Cork in about 1797 and may have fought at Waterloo in 1815 — as a James Derrick served with the Grenadier Guards at that famous battle that ended the Napoleonic Wars. Be that as it may, by 1841 James was recorded on the census as an earthenware dealer living with the Irish family of William Casey in Bilston. Shortly afterwards, he married Eliza Hennessy who was

17

aged about sixteen. Their marriage was short-lived because of his criminality.

In 1849 James was given three months' hard labour at Stafford County Prison for "stealing a quantity of iron from the whimsy of a coal pit". A year later, this conviction was taken into account when he was found guilty of stealing the mill brasses from a mine at Sedgley and sentenced to transportation to Australia. James Derrick was sent to Millbank Prison in London, and then Shorncliffe Prison in Kent. In the latter's Register for 1851, he is described as of sallow complexion with dark hair and grey eyes. He was short, at 5 feet 4½ inches, slender of build and had large thin ears and open nostrils.

His right thumb was broken and his face was pock pitted, suggesting that he had suffered smallpox or some other nasty disease. Married with three children and a Roman Catholic, James could neither read nor write. A labourer by occupation, strangely his character was given as good.

After almost six months at Shorncliffe, James was not transported; instead he was transferred to Dartmoor in Devon and was released on licence in 1855. He seems to have had some contact with his daughter, Bridget, as a decade later she gave him as a labourer on her marriage certificate. Moreover, she and her husband lived in Canal Street, Wolverhampton as did James himself.

He died in 1872, in the Wolverhampton Workhouse. A lonely figure, as much because of his own faults as because of misfortune, for most of his life James

Derrick seems to have lived a life that was out of place and on the margins. Now in death he was cast out beyond the margins. A pauper he was buried in a public grave with other paupers and with no headstone to mark that he had ever lived.

What had happened to my great, great, great grandmother, Eliza, and her children after James had been sent to prison? Soon after that, in October 1850, she was sentenced to six months' hard labour for stealing, and her children were put into the Wolverhampton Union Workhouse. My great, great grandfather, John, was six. His mother went on to marry a William Casey — so perhaps she and James had not been legally married. By 1861 she was a widow with four children aged under eight and was in the Walsall Workhouse.

Interestingly, the Census of that year recorded her son, and my great, great grandfather, John Derrick, as a fifteen-year old living on his own and fending for himself at 181, Cock Street, Darlaston. He was an iron stone miner. Ten years later John had moved to Birmingham and was living in Hurst Street — close to the present National Trust Back to Back Museum.

A telegraph pole worker he was lodging with Edward Thompson and his widowed daughter, Catherine. A few months later, John and Catherine married at St Andrew's Church of England in Bordesley and by 1881 they were living in a back-to-back up a yard in Mole Street, Sparkbrook. With them were Catherine's daughter from her first marriage; their daughter, Flora aged six; and their sons, John nine, James four, and my great grandfather, Edward, two. He and John would soon gain criminal records.

In February 1891, the *Birmingham Daily Post* remarked that at the Balsall Heath Police Court, John Derrick aged 20 had been charged with assaulting a police constable in Thomas Street (later part of Highgate Road, Sparkbrook). This was during the times of the sloggers and the early days of the peaky blinders and John was obviously one of them. A labourer and then living with his family in Emily Street in Highgate, he "was well known to the police authorities as belonging to a gang of roughs who are constantly creating disturbances in Sparkbrook".

On January 31, John had been one of a gang causing a row and when Police Constable Wragge had tried to stop it and take one of the offenders into custody, John Derrick had thrown a brick at him. Inspector Harrison told the magistrates that the prisoner was "a constant source of annoyance as one of the leaders of the rowdies of the district". He was given six weeks in jail.

By then, John's younger brother, Edward aged eleven, was in the Penn Street Industrial School, which was actually in Allcock Street, Deritend close to Heath Mill Lane. In 1857 the Industrial Schools Act had given magistrates the power to sentence children between the ages of seven and fourteen years old to one of these institutions if they were homeless. Four years later the categories were extended to include boys under fourteen who had committed an offence punishable by imprisonment or whose parents could not control them.

According to Mr G. B. Davis, clerk to the Birmingham School Board, "an industrial school child should be one who is not yet a little criminal or does not deserve the name, though he may have committed little acts which are technically crimes. He is a child in bad circumstances who needs to be saved from his surroundings." Sadly Penn Street Industrial School failed with my great grandfather. In 1893 he was convicted of vagrancy and in October 1894, he served seven days in prison for stealing five loaves. Just weeks later, the *Birmingham Daily Post* reported that the sixteen-year-old Edward Derrick had been sentenced to four months' hard labour for burglary.

Then in 1897, he was sent down for five months and handed a two-year supervision order for stealing a bicycle. He was not out of prison long before he was convicted of using obscene language, after which he was imprisoned for twelve months in October 1898 for breaking into a counting house. Police records indicate that he was 5 foot 3½ inches tall, had a blue mark on the back of one forearm and wrist, and a tattoo of a mermaid on the back of the other forearm.

Now a serial offender, in 1899 Edward assaulted a police constable; in 1900 he was arrested for drunkenness; and in October 1901 at Stafford, and under the alias of Fredrick Pitt, he was sent away for three years for bodily harm. Finally in October 1906, he was sentenced to two months' hard labour for stealing a basket carriage from a widow.

A year later, Edward Derrick married my great grandmother, Ada Weldon, at Christ Church, Sparkbrook.

He gave himself as a bricklayer, although previously he had stated he was a tailor and he would later be described as a scrap iron dealer and a rag and bone man. Ada had been born in the very poor Park Street by the Bull Ring. She now worked in a warehouse and lived with her older and younger sisters with their mother and her second husband in Vaughton Street, Highgate.

After her wedding, Ada went to live at 23, Studley Street, just a few yards from Edward's brother, James, who rented a back house in Sills Buildings. But marriage did not change Edward for the better. When I was researching my doctoral thesis in the early 1980s, I spoke with Lil Preston who had lived in the same yard as him, his wife Ada and his daughter, Maisy — my grandmother. She recalled that Edward was a violent man who often smashed up his home when he was drunk and that on occasions Ada and Maisy had to sleep in the brewus (communal washhouse) in the yard or hide from him in the house of her grandmother, the well-loved Granny Carey.

There was a story in our family that Ada went on to divorce Edward Derrick after he had left her. I had always doubted this, thinking that it was too expensive for a working-class person to be able to afford the high costs of a divorce. I was wrong. Ada did get a divorce in 1922 and was able to do so as "a poor person" under the rules of the Supreme Court. She was unable to sign any of her statements and had to make her mark in the presence of a commissioner for oaths.

The divorce documents confirm that from the summer of 1913, Edward Derrick had failed to provide food or clothing for his wife and child. They got by on her wages as a press worker in the brass trade. Then in April 1915 he violently assaulted Ada and threatened to kill her at her house at 25, Studley Street. Six months later, Edward physically attacked his wife with his fist and caused her bodily harm.

It was emphasised that "he had frequently given way to drink and had used foul and abusive language" towards Ada, and that "he has frequently smashed various articles of furniture and has broken up two homes". Thankfully from January 1916, he deserted his wife and daughter and he then moved to Brewery Street, Coventry to live with a widow called Mrs Murphy.

Peakies like my great grandfather, Edward Derrick, and peaky blinders and sloggers like his brother, John, were hooligans who fought each other, assaulted others and were engaged in petty crime. There is no evidence that they were involved in protection rackets. However one man who may well have been a peaky blinder did go on to control the protection rackets on the racecourses of England immediately after the First World War and to become the most powerful gangster in England for a short time. He did so by leading the feared Birmingham or Brummagem Gang and their allies from London, the Elephant Boys and Camden Town Mob. His name was Billy Kimber.

CHAPTER
TWO

The Brummagem Boys

The appearance of the notorious "Boys" from Brummagem was dreaded by racegoers at the little meetings that abounded across England. It was with no wonder, for they were violent men who stole from onlookers who had come to bet on horse racing and who extorted protection money from bookmakers. Major Fairfax-Blakeborough, a distinguished writer on all things to do with "the Turf", declared that by the 1880s "the Birmingham Boys had so lost all honour, decency, and all idea of anything but robbery, that they became a real menace".

Feared as "desperate, dangerous, daredevil fellows", he recounted in the *Sunday Mercury* on January 13, 1935 that on one occasion their arrival in force at Scarborough, with their allies from Leeds, "created such alarm that they were collected by the police before racing commenced, marched down to the railway station, put on to the next train for home and sent off". But the Brummagem Boys never forgot when they had been bested and always gained a bloody revenge. In 1893, and again with their bully-boy mates from Leeds, they returned to the Yorkshire sea-side town and caused mayhem. In a well-organised attack, some of them stormed the turnstiles to the main enclosure and stole all the day's takings.

The few police officers on duty were overwhelmed and dozens of ruffians also climbed over the rails which divided the course from the paddock. They then took watches and money from spectators and "held up" bookmakers. Tom Devereux was one of them. He told Fairfax-Blakeborough that "men were laid out with stakes and empty bottles the length of the enclosure". Another appalled eye-witness exclaimed that "for some ten minutes utter lawlessness prevailed"; whilst police reinforcements were slow in arriving because the course was three miles from the town and at the top of a very steep hill.

The Brummagem Gang were as well-organised in their escape as in their attack. They seemed to vanish into thin air. Not one of them left by train from Scarborough and none arrived back in Birmingham, where the police were waiting for them. With no motorised transport available then, it is thought that the gangsters made their own ways to Derby, where there was racing a couple of days later. There they divided their spoils.

This "raid" forced the closure of Scarborough races — a fate which had also befallen Hall Green and Sutton Coldfield Races because of the depredations of the Brummagem Boys. Five years later their infamy was brought to national attention. There was increasing concern about "roughs on the turf" and on August 13, 1898 a reporter from *The Daily Telegraph* related the evidence from an official who had been involved in trying to deal with ruffianism. He noted that "it is a curious fact that while crime generally has decreased throughout the country, yet there is no diminution of it at race meetings".

The largest number of roughs and thieves "come from Birmingham, and some of them are of the lowest type possible. The "Brums", like the rest of their fraternity, work in gangs of six, seven, and eight — never separating." This organised ruffianism made it hard to deal with. In particular the criminals surrounded and tripped up their victims to rob them, or snatched purses, and watches and chains. And on the way to and from the racecourse by train, they worked the three card trick upon gullible fellow passengers.

The plundering and infamy of the small gangs that were collectively known as the Brummagem Boys were long-standing, although it was rare for them to come together in such force as they had done at Scarborough. In 1856, a local newspaper recounted how the annual Birmingham steeple chases had been moved from Aston on account of "the disorderly and disgraceful conduct of a large number of Birmingham worthies expressively denominated 'roughs'." The new venue was Knowle, because it was felt to be less easy of access. It was a wrong assumption to make.

Thousands of people came from Birmingham in monster excursions along the Great Western Line, in horse-drawn omnibuses and in vehicles of almost every description. Amongst them were "hosts of thimble-riggers, cardsharpers, and other 'professionals' of that delectable genus who infested the course". Not a policeman was to be seen and "order was preserved as well as it could be by a few solitary amateur preservers of the peace; and the pickpockets, who mustered in goodly numbers, profited immensely".

The Brummagem Boys did not restrict their criminality to local racecourses; quickly they began to operate on a regional scale. A year after the disgraceful goings-on at Knowle, the *Derby Mercury* mentioned on September 16, 1857 that Michael Dowling and Michael Lawley had come to Derby by special train from Birmingham for the races the previous day. They had been arrested for pickpocketing at the course and each was sentenced to one month's hard labour.

By the summer of 1871, so notorious were the "boys" from Brummagem that the *East London Observer* pointed out that the recent races at Oxford had afforded "the thieves and welshers of the metropolis, Birmingham &c. an excellent opportunity to enrich themselves at the expense of the public, numberless cases of robbery and welshing having occurred both in and out of the ring".

Four years later, on April 6, 1875, the *Cheltenham Chronicle* related that two Birmingham men had been charged with attempting to pick pockets at the local racecourse. A detective from the city informed the court that Charles Hemmings of Five Ways and George Wallace of Dale End "were in the habit of going about the various race meetings picking pockets, and had been in custody on the charge several times".

They were each sentenced to three months' imprisonment. At the same court, George Wilson of Lichfield Road, Aston was charged with loitering with intent to commit a felony at the Midland Railway station. Described as a betting man, he was "the associate of a gang of thieves in Birmingham". The bench discharged the case but warned Wilson that if he were seen again loitering in the town he would be punished severely.

Then on May 9, 1881, the *Birmingham Daily Post* reported on several cases of gambling and robbery perpetrated by Birmingham men at Stratford Races. Henry Thomas of Godwin Street, was given 28 days' hard labour for stealing a pocket book; so too was Thomas Shelton of Cross Street, in his case for possessing a gambling machine that was misnamed "Billy Fairplay".

A third man, Thomas Holloway, alias Meadows and of Drury Lane, was sent to the assizes for stealing the tickets given to punters by bookmakers. He was damned by Detective Sergeant Orr of the Birmingham force as one of the worst characters in the city. He had spent half of his life in jail and had sixteen previous convictions, some of which were of a very serious nature.

Thomas Osborne of Masshouse Lane was also charged with stealing betting tickets and was handed 28 days' hard labour; whilst James Waldron, William Williams and William Warner, all of Birmingham, were each imprisoned for fourteen days for frequenting the streets with intent to commit a felony. Warner was condemned by detective Sergeant Orr and another Birmingham policeman as "one of the worst thieves in Birmingham".

Three men were also charged with cardsharping on the highway. They were William Martin alias College of Windmill Street, who had thirteen previous convictions and was given three months' hard labour; James Edwards of Barford Street; and James Henry Leek of Canal Street, the self-styled "King of the Card Sharpers". Each was sentenced to a month in prison. All the money found on the trio of tricksters was ordered to be used for their maintenance whilst in prison.

Leek continued with his trickery for at least the next two decades. On May 10, 1902 the *Manchester Courier and Lancashire General Advertiser* described him as a general dealer living in Price Street in the Gun Quarter who had been arrested at the Chester Races for gaming with cards. A detective from Birmingham said that Leek was one of the ringleaders of cardsharpers in the city and that he generally carried the money and financed the others. Indeed he was still called "King of the Sharpers". He was sentenced to one month's hard labour.

The ongoing problems caused by thieves from Birmingham were emphasised on May 19, 1887 when the *Bath Chronicle and Weekly Gazette* informed its readers that a gang of about fourteen cardsharpers from the town had arrived the day before for the Bath and Somerset County Races. A few days previously, five Birmingham men had been charged as suspected persons and reputed thieves with being at Shrub Hill Station in Worcester with intent to commit a felony. The *Birmingham Daily Post* of May 13 stated that they had arrived in the city to go to the races but were apprehended by the city's Chief Constable. He had been accompanied by a detective from the Birmingham police, who had gone to the station to prevent pickpockets from plying their nefarious calling.

Of course, gangs of thieves from Liverpool, Manchester, Sheffield, Nottingham and various parts of London were also active in their regional racecourses. But like those from the capital, it seems the Birmingham criminals were determined to operate not only within their acknowledged sphere of control in the Midlands and the West Country but also further afield. Such criminality was enabled by relatively cheap travel on the English rail network and of course, the place to travel to for the richest pickings was London.

In the autumn of 1890 the *Sheffield Daily Telegraph* carried an intriguing article on "London's Cleverest Little Pickpocket". James Carney was "a diminutive specimen of humanity, whose head barely reached the height of the dock rail at the Southwark Police Court" on November 3. He was appearing there because he had thrown a cup of hot coffee over a young lady without any apparent reason, after which he had behaved in a violent manner and used the most abominable language when he had been apprehended.

Whilst Carney was in the dock he was recognised by a detective sergeant who was at the court on another matter. The officer pointed out that the criminal was "an associate of known thieves, and although he was not yet seventeen, he was the leader of a gang of young thieves known as the 'Brummagem Gang'." A companion of a notorious brothel-house keeper and tutor of young thieves, Carney "was known to the officers of Scotland Yard as the cleverest little pickpocket in London".

The criminal took pleasure in his unsavoury reputation, smiling and gazing at the ceiling. After he was sentenced to 21 days' hard labourer he turned and smiled at a young girl and then "in a very impudent manner jumped out the dock". On his way to the cells, Carney imitated the mannerisms of the detective sergeant "much to the amusement of his fellow prisoners".

For all the attractions of London to pickpockets, racecourses were the places favoured most by them, cardsharpers and chancers of every kind. This was because of the lack of protection for many racegoers and because large crowds afforded safety from detection. In August 1885, the *Daily Telegraph* ran a major feature on the problem of ramps (swindlers) and roughs under the heading "On the Rampage". Calling himself "one of the crowd", the journalist travelled by train to a big meeting with a police inspector. During his travel, he met a company of "unmitigated scoundrels".

They were worse than the usual bully boys as they combined craft with cunning and with unhesitating brutality. Often dressed with a passably decent set of clothes, they were educated well enough to get into affable conversation with anyone they spotted as their prey. Working in small groups of four or five, they stalked winning punters to lift them of their money. If they could not do so stealthily they would resort to violence.

One man called "Beauty Brown" recounted how he and his fellows had "stagged" a chap who, over an afternoon's racing, had won the large sum of £70 — equivalent to a skilled man's wages for a year. The intended victim was alert to the danger he was in and was accompanied by a couple of tall friends. Keeping his hand deep in his pocket to protect his money, he felt safe — until Beauty Brown stabbed him in the back with a stiff brass pin, pushing it in to the head. The injured man yelled and pulled his hand out of his pocket whereupon it was picked swiftly and expertly.

It was the rampant criminality at many racecourses that led the *Daily Telegraph* to bemoan the ruffianism on the turf in a number of high-profile articles in 1898. The point was made in the *Newcastle Journal* on August 29 of that year that this was by no means a novel topic for "all the chief sporting papers have been hammering at it from time to time at any period over the last twenty years". Moreover ruffianism was not "a special disease peculiar to race meetings".

Like thieving, picking pockets and highway robbery in broad daylight it was a form of roguery that could be found wherever people gathered in large numbers. But if it was unfair to speak of racecourse ruffianism as if it were "an especially wicked and exclusive case of crime", it was fair to assert that "at race meetings the pick-pocket, rogue, blackguard and rough have a greater chance than at other assemblages". This was because "the law in its wisdom refuses the protection to race meetings that it gives to other gatherings".

The Jockey Club was the official governing body for horse racing in Britain and its stewards were often blamed for the widespread criminality on racecourses. But "what can the Jockey Club do? They have no power given to them to legally arrest or interfere with men behaving badly". The writer for the *Newcastle Journal* compared this unhappy situation with that of railway companies, which had special bye-laws to keep their trains, platforms, stations and premises free of obnoxious characters and law breakers. No such power was vested in racing authorities. In the absence of Government action to address this problem then lawlessness on racecourses continued to grow — and was facilitated by the layout at racecourses.

When Sandown Park opened in 1875, it was the first enclosed course in the country. This meant that its management could more easily charge an entry fee. Thereafter more and more courses were enclosed, and each was then divided into railed off areas for different types of spectator according to their social status and income. At the most popular of them, the wealthiest racegoers stood in the members' enclosure, in which bookmakers were not allowed to stand and take bets.

Instead they lined the other side of the rails that cordoned off the members' enclosure, shouting the odds across to potential punters. These bookmakers were in Tattersall's Ring but took bets on credit; whereas the other bookies in that ring, and elsewhere, accepted only ready cash.

Tattersall's was the most expensive enclosure for non-members. Next came the silver ring. As its name suggests, this was cheaper to enter and like the onlookers, the bookmakers here were not as prosperous. Harry Denton was a silver-ring bookmaker who died in 1949 and he recalled that at Kempton Park bookies like him "betted on the bottom steps of the stands and all over the Ring, there being no lines or fixed position, but claiming their position by right of usage". And they wore "varied costumes, each man to his own fancy, multi coloured and checked suits with white hats predominating".

In 1896, Julius Symons, then an old man, "favoured the costume of an African explorer with white costume and helmet and he used to stand at the bottom step of the stand in most of the Silver Rings". Another well-known character was George Lill. His motto was "to win and 1, 2, 3" and he wore an antiquated frock coat and top hat. As for Morey and Janey Marks, they called themselves "Our Boys" and dressed as midshipmen. In the 1880s they took a lifeboat with them to attract custom at Epsom Downs on Derby Day.

Finally many racegoers who could not afford to pay for the silver ring stood for free in open areas known as "outside", where there were also bookies keen to take bets. According to the *Sheffield Daily Telegraph* of August 13, 1892 "once in Tattersall's ring you are safe" but to slightly paraphrase a popular ditty, "It's alright when you get there but you've got to get there first". And what was more "you've got to get way into the bargain and that's exactly what you very often can't do".

Despite these problems, on July 23, 1892 the *Yorkshire Gazette* stressed that the Jockey Club took very good care of Tattersall's enclosure, from which "at most of the crack meetings, welshers and thieves are vigorously excluded". By contrast the cheap rings at all race meetings were managed in a wretched manner so that patrons of the silver rings were robbed in open daylight. And pickpockets and thugs were not the only thieves — so too were those who claimed to be bookmakers but in reality were "welshers".

Fairfax-Blakeborough wrote that this name arose from David Welch, a pioneer bookmaker about whom it was said that he never paid out to winning clients. Whatever its origins, welshers were despicable. In his memoirs, *Leaves from a Bookmaker's Book* (1931), Thomas Henry Dey described the modus operandi of a gang of welshers who operated on a big scale. One of them stood up to make a book and took the money for the bets from the public. This was handed at intervals "to a confederate, so that when the bookmaker is ready to vamoose, he has practically no money on him, and, in consequence, is more or less in a position to plead mistaken identity if caught. The money is subsequently divided between the confederates."

If the welsher was not able to escape readily and there was a rumpus then his sidekicks would make themselves useful in some way or other, either in protecting the villain, or by interfering with those who were attempting to wreak their vengeance on him, or by mixing with the crowd and pretending also to be victims, leading the public on a false scent, even, if necessity arises, resorting to force in their endeavours to protect their comrade.

There was another form of welshing known as "ringing the book". Simply any big wagers were booked to a horse different from the one that was really backed. If that horse lost then, of course, the punter made no claim; if it won, then the entry written in the book by the bookmaker's clerk would be shown, and there was "generally a confederate to substantiate the bookmaker's word". In these circumstances no help could be given to the duped customer by a policeman or an official of the ring.

Dyke Wilkinson was a colourful Birmingham character who was involved in a number of business schemes but most of all was magnetised by horse racing. He lost large sums to his passion both as a professional bettor and a racecourse bookmaker, which he took up in 1865. He argued that whilst there had always been welshers, a new type emerged from the 1870s.

They came not in single file "but in whole battalions, terrorising the ring, and setting all lawful authorities at defiance. It would seem as though the good news had been conveyed to the purlieus of thievery in all our great cities that here was a field of labour for the thief, where to ply his occupation in broad daylight, and in sight of the very guardians of the law, without fear of interference."

Wilkinson himself was viciously beaten and maimed by welshers and later witnessed the horrible assault on an elderly and feeble man who had fallen victim to ringing the book at Lichfield Races. A firm of welshers had established themselves in the ring and:

> the ruffian who acted the part of bookmaker was perched on the top of a high stool. He had hung round his neck, by means of a broad yellow strap, a large satchel, on the front of which was emblazoned, in gold letters, the name of one of the best-known bookmakers. This, by-the-by, was a very common practice, and, in more than one case I have known respectable bookmakers permit their names to be forged ill this way, and the public thereby gulled, because they were afraid of the consequences to themselves if they interfered.

The respectable old gentleman approached the bookmaker's joint to claim his winnings of £14. Wilkinson stated that an old-fashioned welsher would have already fled with his takings, but "not so with the modern type of welsher, he maintained his position with an effrontery bred of constant success". The punter was told that he had not backed the winner, his ticket was torn up and he was warned to go away.

Most people would have been scared off by "the savage demeanour of this bookmaker, supplemented as it was by the rude and uncomplimentary remarks of a little band of square-headed ruffians by whom he was immediately surrounded. But this old gentleman, with more valour than discretion, was not of that metal."

An excitable and passionate little man, he began a violent argument, "and when he found himself being hustled about by those surrounding him he made a snatch at the satchel, which was the signal for 'the boys' to begin their work". In a minute, "the poor old man was kicked into unconsciousness, his pockets rifled of watch and money, and I have no doubt that, although no bones were broken, he had received injuries which would trouble him as long as he lived, and probably shorten his life." As for the welsher and his confederates, they got clear away to continue their business elsewhere.

"The boys" was the generic term for the ruffians who were the curse of racecourses and as Wilkinson asserted, their numbers rose towards the end of the nineteenth century because of the rich and easy pickings for their criminality. Attendances were increasing as more courses put on exciting and often shorter races such as sprints and handicaps on the Flat and not over jumps.

This rise was facilitated by two other factors: first, better transport links because of the development of railway networks; and second, by cheap local evening newspapers and daily sporting publications like the *Sporting Life* and *Sporting Chronicle* which provided racing information and tips. Moreover the attraction of betting on a racecourse was enhanced because it was legal. By comparison betting for cash off course was against the law and would not be legalised until 1961 when lawful betting shops opened for the first time.

The upsurge in attendances was most marked in the London area, where, from the 1860s, there was an increase in the number of meetings. Fairfax-Blakeborough, in an article in 1951 in the bookmaker's publication *Banyan*, emphasised that this brought with it "a flood of bookmaker's of mushroom growth, and of no stability, whose conduct did much to bring these fixtures, racing and the bookmaking profession into ill-repute". But increasingly "the boys" also targeted bookmakers for protection money. In his *Turf Memories of Sixty years* (1925), Alex Scott noted that to protect themselves from intimidation, many layers employed "minders".

The first definite breakaway from this astounding state of affairs was the hiring of:

professional pugilists by the bookmakers to protect their persons from violence and their pockets from the tribute demanded by "the boys". Paradoxical though it may seem nowadays, it was the straight men among the ready-money bookmakers of the 'seventies, 'eighties, and 'nineties who had well-known boxers standing beside them while they transacted their business. Popular imagination, of course, always credited the bookmaker's escort with being there to silence dissatisfied punters instead of protecting his employer from "the boys". George Gurney, one of the big ready-money men in the 'seventies and 'eighties, employed Bob Travers, the "negro" fighter, and afterwards Nunc Wallace, to act as protectors.

Unfortunately for the good reputation of book-making, Scott was correct to identify a negative response to the employment of minders. In 1905, an article in the *Birmingham Mail* stated that if a man's character was to be known by the company he keeps, "then the bookmaker stands condemned at once". The writer declared that "a more villainous-looking horde than the 'bookie's' retinue would be hard to find". They were "vulgar in their attire, cunning — in many cases criminal — in features, loud-mouthed, and filthy. Many of them were 'discredited prize-fighters' who came in useful when their bosses wanted to take over a favoured pitch, or else, if they wished to 'pacify' an obstreperous client."

By the early twentieth century, many parts of English racecourses were lawless places where might was right and the most frightening collection of gangs that marauded across them was known collectively as the Brummagem Boys. On August 22, 1898, a commentator in the *Glasgow Herald* observed that their freedom to rob and bully was most marked in racecourses that were in the hands of amateurs. He amplified by using the new racecourse at Folkestone as his example.

It was a steeplechase, a form of racing that unusually was more popular in Kent than was the Flat. Such a new meeting "was the happy hunting ground of thieves and welshers, more especially of what is known as the 'Birmingham Division'". Local policemen had been placed on all the gates of entry. They were very good men for ordinary police work but "they were altogether at sea for dealing with wily welshers". These had come down in large numbers and were "furnished with yellow discs on which were stamped 'Reserved Enclosure' and with this they went all over the place". Moreover, many robberies were committed on the approaches to the railway station.

The loose collection of gangs from Birmingham included cardsharpers and these Brummagem Boys also turned their attention to other events where large crowds gathered. On May 25, 1907, the *Cheltenham Chronicle and Gloucestershire Graphic* reported that the local police were keeping "a smart lookout upon the doings of a gang of Birmingham gamblers who infest the various sporting fixtures in the Midlands, and are persistent in paying their attentions to Cheltenham". Cardsharpers who had operated at the steeplechase races had already been convicted and, following a number of other sports events on the previous Easter Monday, "some smart fines were inflicted upon several of this gentry".

Two years later, on May 8, 1909, the *Manchester Courier and Lancashire General Advertiser* announced that William Downes and George Wright were "notorious Birmingham thieves and pickpockets". The previous day each of them had been sentenced to three months' imprisonment for frequenting Watergate Street in Chester on the Cup Day of the races. In particular, a detective reported that Downes had "piloted all the crowds of thieves that were sent to the city".

Fairfax-Blakeborough noted that the majority of these Brummagem Boys "were men of broken-nosed, cauliflower-eared type, with crime written on their faces". There was an exception. In the 1890s, one of their leaders was "a tall, good-looking man who always dressed well, spoke with a cultured voice, and would pass as a gentleman anywhere".

This man was known by sight by all regular racing men, stayed at the best hotels, played a good game of billiards and cards, and paid up whenever he lost. He stood his corner, never asked for information about horses, always had plenty of money and did not bet much. However it was eventually believed that he was responsible for some hotel robberies of men staying in them who had won considerable sums at betting at the races.

Whether this man was arrested, convicted abroad or gave up the game was not known, but his identity remained a mystery; however just before the First World War, a figure emerged who was to become the leader of the Brummagem Boys and who would bring them together in a firmer grouping allied to the feared Elephant Boys of South London. His name was Billy Kimber — but before he did so a vicious gang war erupted in Birmingham. It involved men who were castigated as racecourse pests and one would become a dreaded associate of Kimber on the racecourses of England. This gang war is recalled in the city's working-class folklore as the Garrison Lane Vendetta.

CHAPTER
THREE

The Garrison Lane Vendetta

Hereditary family blood feuds were ingrained upon the hearts of the people of Corsica — or so it seemed for many acclaimed and well-read French authors. From Honoré de Balzac's *The Vendetta* of 1830 to Guy de Maupassant's *The Corsican Bandit* of 1877, the idea of Corsica as a place where the vengeful killing was a way of life and death captured the popular imagination in France — and soon it swiftly caught hold in Britain.

Here, however, vendettas came to be regarded as something inherent not only to the people of Corsica but also to those of southern Italy and nearby islands. The emergence of the new expression into the English language owed much to the great Charles Dickens and his weekly literary magazine *All the Year Round*. In July 1860 he included an article on Sardinia in which was mentioned "the lingering influence of the deadly 'vendetta' — inherited blood-feud — which has sacrificed whole families, and once depopulated an entire village for one girl".

Derived from the Latin term "vindicta", meaning vengeance, the word vendetta would soon be associated not only with bloody feuds in the Mediterranean but also with those in the back streets of Birmingham. In March 1890, the "Grand Theatre" in Corporation Street put on the comic opera *Paola; or the Vendetta*. Set in eighteenth-century Corsica, its plot was woven around the tale of a centuries'-old violent hostility between two families. Strangely, just the next year, on June 11, the *Birmingham Daily Post* reported on a vicious assault upon Thomas Reynolds by a George Gower, explaining that the victim appeared to be the subject "of some sort of vendetta".

Reynolds had previously given evidence against some men for the theft of a bag containing £200. Since their conviction, their companions, who met at a pub in Beak Street off Severn Street, had declared that they would gain vengeance. The unfortunate Reynolds was then attacked with a knife by a "notorious ruffian" called Kennealy and was kicked unmercifully by others. Kennealy was arrested and sent to prison for two months. On the evening of the court's decision, the luckless Reynolds was in Temple Row when Gower came upon him, "and having abused him, kicked him, felled him to the ground, resumed his kicking, and finally ran away".

The Stipendiary Magistrate was rightfully disgusted by what had happened. He declared that "it was time that this sort of thing was stopped. It was a disgrace to the city, and he meant putting an end to it." Unhappily he was unable to do so, for a decade later in the summer of 1901, the "Birmingham Slum Vendetta" gained attention in newspapers across the land. On June 14, the *Northampton Mercury* stated that a labourer called John Joyce, aged 42 and nicknamed Toby, had been found guilty by a coroner's jury of the wilful murder of a cobbler named John Nugent who was 61.

Joyce had been "at loggerheads" with the Nugent family for two years. Indeed he and the murdered man's son, Michael, "had numerous severe fights with weapons of all kinds". According to the *Dundee Courier* of August 1, "it was notorious that there was bad blood between them" and Michael Nugent had been charged with unlawfully wounding Joyce with a bayonet but had been discharged. The newspapers related that the younger Nugent was now in a lunatic asylum, but Joyce continued the feud.

On the day of the killing, premeditation was suggested by that fact that he had been hanging about the court (yard of back-to-back houses) in which the deceased lived for three hours before the murder was committed. When Joyce saw the elder Nugent, he stabbed him in the heart with a knife. The defence stated that the wounding had been accidental; whilst the jury asked for mercy because they believed that Joyce's "head had been affected by the sun and fever whilst serving as a corporal in India". Despite this plea Joyce was sentenced to be hanged at the Birmingham Assizes on July 31. Then on August 17, 1901, the *Manchester Evening News* noted that the Home Secretary had decided not to interfere with the due course of the law in the case. Consequently Joyce was executed on the following Tuesday.

As for Michael Nugent, he was a deeply troubled man. Court records indicate that in 1885 and when he was just eleven, he was sent to reformatory school for five years for stealing a silk handkerchief. After his release he was arrested and imprisoned on numerous occasions for assault or theft. Then in December 1901, a few months after the murder of his father, he was sent down for three months for attempted suicide. He would try to take his life again in 1907, when he lay across a railway line. This time he was punished with six months' jail — a term he was also sentenced to in 1911 when he once more sought to commit suicide.

Thirty-five years after the "Birmingham Slum Vendetta", another vicious outbreak of vengeance in Birmingham's back streets gained notoriety. On Tuesday November 17, 1936 the *Gloucester Citizen* carried on its front page the headline "Assaults by 'Toughs' Alleged Vendetta Incidents". The report emphasised that "allegations of assaults by a gang of 'toughs', the use of brick and heavy pieces of lead piping as weapons, and the terrorisation of a district by clashes in the course of a vendetta, were made at Birmingham today".

Lewis Slater, aged 43 and a mantle maker from Darwin Street, his son, David, also from Darwin Street, and Thomas Shaw of Charles Henry Street were remanded on bail for a week. They were charged with "assault, making use of threats, and doing wilful damage". A detective said that "there appeared to have been a vendetta in the Darwin Street neighbourhood

47

for some time, and the Slaters' house was smashed up on three successive nights".

A man called William Street, also of Darwin Street, had his ribs broken and was now in hospital. A remand was granted upon the application of Mr A. J. Hatwell, appearing for the Slaters, who made it plain that they intended to take proceedings against Street for unlawful wounding. Mr Hatwell emphasised that it was contrary to his instructions that the Slaters had terrorised the district. Quite the opposite, in fact, as "they had the police in the house for protection last night but after the officers had gone a gang of 'toughs' set about them and a brick had been thrown through the window".

Two years before the victimisation of the Street family, the most notorious vendetta in Birmingham's history was alluded to in a disturbing Birmingham case that was brought to notice on the front page of the *Gloucestershire Echo*. The headline ran, "Weird weapons in Court. Pistols with Knife Blade and Weights. Alleged Threat to Murder Wife." The story recounted was that of William Jones. Aged 70, he was a tinplate worker who lived in Eversley Road, Small Heath and he was charged with threatening to murder his wife and with having two revolvers without certificates.

Detective Sergeant Cross told the magistrates that Jones had come to the police station to complain that someone had broken into his house, forced a box and taken a revolver that was within it. When the police went to the home, Mrs Jones explained that she had broken into the box and taken the two revolvers inside it as her husband had held one of them in his hand and threatened to kill her.

It was then discovered that Jones had "an amazing collection of weird lethal weapons". It included a walking stick to which was attached a wire with a weight on so that the stick could be swung around. At its end was a spike. Another walking stick had a long stick at the end so that it could be used like a bayonet. It was also armed with protruding nails so that if it were seized the nails would stick in the opponent's hands. Then there was a metal tube for discharging sand or pepper. Additionally, it was fitted with a number of spikes at the end so that if the attack failed the opponent's hand would run into the spikes.

Finally there were three guns. One was a home-made pistol from which pepper or sand could be discharged, whilst pressure on the trigger released a knife blade. A wire weighted with lead was also attached to this weapon. A second revolver was fitted with three blades which sprung out when triggered. The upper one might be used as a bayonet and the lower one was hooked as if for ripping. This gun was loaded with two ball cartridges; whilst the third was charged with wads, pepper and a blank cartridge.

The police officer suggested that he thought that Jones was a case for the doctor. Jones, however, stated that "he was given the small pistol to take care of when a vendetta was on in Garrison Lane, Birmingham 24 years ago". This Garrison Lane Vendetta was remembered for many years because of its viciousness and endurance. Born in 1897 and raised in

Sparkbrook, my Great Uncle Wal wrote up some of his memories towards the end of his life and he affirmed that "notorious were the gangs of Garrison Lane and Summer Lane, the former carrying on a vendetta existing over many years".

It was the practice to team up after a session of beer drinking, after getting equipped with knuckledusters, buckled belts, and other weapons, to make for the locality of the rival gang that had a "dust up" owing to them, when invariably it meant a set-to when no quarter was asked or given. Birmingham was not alone in this gang warfare, happening also in many of the big cities, eventually calling for stern measures to cope with it.

This Garrison Lane Vendetta involved riots, shootings and fierce fights and was fought between the Sheldon and Beach families and their respective allies.

The Sheldon brothers had a bad reputation in and around Bordesley and Deritend. It was well deserved, for they were violent men who had no shame in beating the weak — as the unfortunate O'Neills knew all too well. One night in early November 1895, Thomas O'Neill had been coming out of the Great Western pub in Allcock Street. As he did so he was met by John Sheldon, who shouted, "I have been looking for you". Sheldon then struck his victim with a blow to his head.

O'Neill tried to fight back and closed with Sheldon but was then hit on the head with a heavy buckled belt by William Green, who claimed that he had done so accidentally. Margaret O'Neill, the victim's daughter, disagreed as she had seen the belt swung at her father and had appealed to his attackers not to beat him. Green had then pulled her to the ground by her hair, and whilst she was lying there Sheldon had kicked her.

Both men were found guilty of assault and were sentenced to six weeks' in jail with hard labour. Sheldon himself was aged 29 and living in Palmer Street, but was disapproved of as a loafer. He was a man who got by without working and had done so for all his adult life, having been called a "bad character" when he had been aged just seventeen. On that occasion, in January 1884, he and two other teenagers had been fined for travelling on the train between Birmingham and Coventry without paying for tickets.

In the following years, Sheldon was convicted for vagrancy, obstruction, uttering counterfeit coins, theft and assaults. His brother, Samuel, was cast from the same nasty mould. In 1888, he was nineteen and living in New Bartholomew Street, close to what is now Millennium Point. He gave his occupation as a wire drawer but it is apparent that he did not follow it, for in May of that year he and two others were charged with stealing 30 tins of salmon and three tins of jam from a provision dealer's in New Canal Street.

On that occasion Sheldon was fortunate as the charges were dismissed. Six months later, in November 1888, he stated that he was a nailcaster living in Witton Street, off Garrison Lane. On this occasion he was charged with assaulting police constables Sperrins and Madeley. They told the magistrates at Birmingham

Police Court that a few nights previously they had been involved "in a fierce combat with a gang of roughs in Heath Mill Lane" when "their opponents' force had been augmented by the prisoner and a number of his companions".

The constables managed to arrest some of the ring leaders but were then "assailed more violently than ever". Sheldon followed behind and pelted the police with stones, but realising that he was recognised he ran off. A day or two later he was hunted down by Police Constable Allsop. In the meantime, Sheldon had joined in another attack on the police and had stoned PC Harry Edmunds, "behaving with a violence which knew no bounds".

Though he was young, Sheldon had already been convicted a dozen times for assault and was now sentenced to four months' imprisonment with hard labour. The *Birmingham Daily Post* was pleased that such a rough had been severely punished; but it did not turn him from his path of crime because in November 1889, he was sent to jail for six months for "a disgraceful assault on a girl". Harriet Davis was just sixteen when Sheldon and "some eight or nine other roughs" went to her house in Witton Street. They smashed the windows then followed her upstairs where they "committed a most disgusting assault". The unfortunate girl raised the alarm and a police constable rushed to the scene and arrested Sheldon and two others.

Sheldon was not out of jail for long when, in July 1890, he was convicted of a breach of the peace after assaulting a man in Curzon Street. Five years later, in November 1895, Samuel Sheldon now said that he was a tube drawer living in Palmer Street, when he and his wife, Ellen, were charged with breaking and entering into the premises of a hosier and stealing 30 silk mufflers, 120 silk handkerchiefs, two cardigan jackets and several woollen shirts. Ellen Sheldon then persuaded a young woman from Glover Street to start a club with her workmates to buy some of the handkerchiefs at 2s 6d each. It would have been a profitable enterprise, bringing in £15. Other stolen items were to be sold from the huckster's (small general store) shop run by the Sheldons.

A decade later, in 1900, Ellen Sheldon, May Hubble and Polly Bassett from Great Barr Street were charged with attacking Charlotte Nolan, a neighbour, after she had given evidence against Samuel Sheldon. Once she had left the court, Mrs Nolan was abused in every conceivable way, her eyes were blackened and she was disfigured in other ways after she was kicked on the ground. The prosecuting counsel proclaimed that the three women came from "the most lawless part of Birmingham". The case against Bassett was discharged, whilst Sheldon and Hubble were each fined five shillings (25p).

As for Samuel Sheldon, it is apparent that he had become a career criminal and in 1900 he was one of a number of men, including others from Birmingham, who stole about £112 in gold, silver and cheques from the safe of a Leicester publican. Two years later he was sentenced to fourteen days' hard labour for the theft of a double-barrelled gun and ammunition from a man in Northamptonshire. It would not be long before Samuel Sheldon and his brother, John, would both be involved in serious shooting incidents in the worst and most protracted gang war in Birmingham's history — the Garrison Lane Vendetta.

By the early twentieth century John Sheldon was describing himself as a commission agent. This was a favourite "catch-all" term used by the pickpockets, thugs and fraudsters who preyed upon legitimate bookmakers and punters on racecourses. Indeed in September 1919 Sheldon was one of three Birmingham men arrested at Derby racecourse for fleecing others through the game of spinning jenny. He was fined 40 shillings, and the *Nottingham Evening Post* reported that "he was particularly well-known to the police, there being seventeen previous convictions against him".

It is obvious that Sheldon was one of the many racecourse pests from Birmingham who had gained notoriety since the 1870s. As such he would have had connections to Billy Kimber, the powerful and charismatic Brummie gangster who would take control of the racecourse rackets across England shortly after the Great War. Be that as it may, in early 1906 John Sheldon was charged with "feloniously, unlawfully and maliciously" attempting to discharge a loaded pistol at Police Constable Thomas Mooney with intent to cause grievous bodily harm. He was found not guilty by the jury.

The incident had taken place on Boxing Day 1905. Three days before, Charles Connor had shot at a

54

Thomas Barlow. He was also found not guilty of intending to cause grievous bodily harm. This latter shooting appears to be the first public sign of a vicious feud between the Sheldons and their allies and William Beach and his friends such as Connor.

It seems that the Garrison Lane Vendetta, as it became known, had started when Beach had beaten up one of the Sheldons one night after drinking in a local pub. Terry Lines is William Beach's great grandson and he was told that the fight started over a gambling debt. That would seem plausible. Back in the early 1990s I interviewed a grandson of Billy Beach. He knew little about his grandfather but understood that he had lived in Holmes Buildings, in the Garrison Lane flats, and that the feud was "all about racecourses".

Beach himself had grown up nearby in Palmer Street, in the same neighbourhood as the Sheldons. He still lived there and the two gangs must have been well known to each other. That meant that the opportunities for tit-for-tat beatings and attacks were increased — and that a state of tension dominated the lives of the men and their families. This is emphasised by Terry Lines, whose grandmother on that side, "even after her marriage, slept with a lump hammer under her pillow".

The fights between the two gangs erupted into a full-blown riot on January 1, 1909 when the Sheldons gathered in force to attack Billy Beach. In the aftermath, John Sheldon (43), Charles Loone (33) and Charles Jones (29) were charged with unlawfully and violently assembling to disturb the public peace. With "diverse other persons to the number of 10 or more", they had made "a great riot and disturbance to the terror and alarm of His Majesty's subjects". Sheldon and Jones, who had numerous convictions for theft, drunkenness and assault, were each sentenced to twelve months' in prison with hard labour. Loone was handed a term of eight months.

Beach was quick to gain revenge. Four days later he and his men attacked the Sheldons. This may have been the occasion recalled to me by Beach's grandson when one of the homes of the Sheldons was set on fire and another of their gang was blinded when he was beaten by the bridge in Garrison Lane. Beach was also charged with riot, and was given eight months' hard labour. Aged 29 he was a tube drawer with previous convictions for assault.

Of his accomplices, Thomas Lane (27) was found not guilty but Arthur Morris was imprisoned for twelve months' hard labour. He was 36 and supposedly a bricklayer, but was in fact another hardened criminal. When he had been thirteen he had been sent to industrial school for five years because he was an associate of thieves and he went on to be convicted many times for assault, theft, wounding and other offences.

Shortly after Beach came out of jail, on September 18, 1910, he was shot at by John Sheldon, his brother Joseph Sheldon, Charles Jones and Edward Collins — a very dangerous man with several convictions for assault, wounding and grievous bodily harm. The four of them were found guilty of feloniously and unlawfully wounding Beach with intent to kill him. The Sheldon brothers and Jones were each sentenced to five years with hard labour, whilst Collins was sent down for three years.

Terry Lines recalls how he learned about this shooting from his father "one night in the 1950s as we went to St Andrew's (the Birmingham City ground). As we crossed the road by the old Kingston Cinema there were some men's urinals on the corner of Coventry Road and St Andrews Road. My father stopped me and said, 'see those marks on the brick work, that's where the Sheldons tried to shoot your mom's granddad Billy Beach'. A second cousin also told me they also had a pop at him outside the Sailor's Return."

The Sheldons were now severely weakened by the imprisonment of so many of their gang, all the more so as Samuel was also in jail serving five years for uttering counterfeit coins in 1907. Then in March 1911, Billy Beach was sent back to prison for fourteen months for unlawfully and maliciously wounding two women, Fanny Gosling and Annie Elizabeth Warner. He and Samuel Sheldon came out of jail early in 1912 and the Garrison Lane Vendetta flared up once again.

Early that year, Sheldon was arrested with Thomas Ingram of Heath Mill Lane and Edward Tomkin of Floodgate Street for causing grievous bodily harm to Billy Beach. The three men then cross summonsed Beach for assault. The story goes that the judge told Beach that he had two choices: either go back to prison or emigrate to Canada. He emigrated. Sheldon and Ingram were also brought before the court for assaulting Charles Franklin, one of Beach's friends. It was stated that Franklin had threatened them with a revolver and that Sheldon had taken it off him. Then Ingram slashed Franklin across the face with a blade.

The Garrison Lane Vendetta now made national news after another shooting. On October 15, the *Manchester Guardian* reported that this highlighted a revival in the feuds between rival gangs of roughs resulting in a number of serious cases of wounding. The police declared that the local people lived in a state of terror and that "it is almost impossible to persuade them to give evidence against the offenders owing to their fear".

Even though Beach had gone away, he had left behind lieutenants and at about 9.30p.m. on Saturday October 12 they struck. Charlie Connor, Charlie Franklin, Sammy Morris and Albert Broome confronted Sam Sheldon on his own territory, in the King's Arms in Great Barr Street. He was on his own, as his ally Tommy Ingram had just left. Connor told an acquaintance to leave the pub as it was "going to be on" and then turned to Sheldon and said "hello Baggy" before striking him with a life preserver.

As Sheldon fell forwards, Morris and Franklin quickly took out revolvers from their coat pockets and Franklin shot twice at Sheldon across Morris's shoulder. One bullet went through Sheldon's hat and the other hit him in his temple but fortunately did not kill him. The four assailants then left and Sheldon stood up to finish his drink before he collapsed and was taken to hospital.

58

All four men were arrested swiftly and found guilty of intent to murder at Birmingham Assizes early in December. Mr Justice Scrutton explained that in 1910 Mr Justice Bucknill had passed long terms of imprisonment on the Sheldons to give "the inhabitants of the neighbourhood a warning that unless they halted their ways heavier sentences would be passed until they were induced to become law-abiding subjects of the King".

This warning had not been heeded and so now Franklin was imprisoned for ten years; Connor for five years; Morris for four years; and Broome, Franklin's brother-in-law, for three years. On appeal Connor's term was reduced to three years for grievous bodily harm. Thus ended the notorious Garrison Lane Vendetta.

Thereafter John Sheldon continued to live as "a racecourse pest" and on September 3, 1919 the *Derby Evening Telegraph* noted that he had been fined 40 shillings for gaming with a spinning jenny at Derby Races. His enemy Charlie Franklin of the Beach Gang would become a leading figure in the Birmingham Gang in the racecourse wars with the Sabinis of London. By contrast, Terry Lines has found that William Beach "joined the Canadian Overseas Volunteer Force on September 23, 1914 where he says he was 35 years old and had served five years in 6th Battalion of the Warwickshire Regiment. He survived the First World War as on January 24, 1924 he moved from Canada to Detroit in Michigan as we have him being recorded going through the border crossing in Quebec."

CHAPTER
FOUR

Billy Kimber's Rise

Billy Kimber was not a man to be crossed. Tall, powerfully built, strong and charismatic, he feared no man but many men feared him. A tough fighter himself, he was the key figure in a group of vicious and frightening thugs called variously the Birmingham Gang, the Brummagem Gang and the Brummagem Boys. Drawn from across the city, these were not teenaged hooligans; rather they were dangerous men who had long led lives dominated by fighting, pick pocketing and intimidation. In the brief boom that followed the end of the First World War, this Birmingham Gang controlled the protection rackets on the racecourses of England and made huge sums of money.

From 1920 their supremacy in the south was challenged by the Sabini Gang of London but neither Kimber nor the rest of the Birmingham Gang were prepared to give up their over-lordship of lucrative courses like Epsom. In the resultant racing-gang feud, men were killed and others seriously wounded by the shooting of revolvers or with knives, cut-throat razors and other weapons.

That vendetta was not surprising, as men from both sides were steeped in violence, William Kimber amongst them. He was born in 1882 in Number 55 Court in Summer Lane. His mother was Catherine, nee Farrell, and his father, also William, was a brass founder. Both had been born in Birmingham and they had lived in this yard of back-to-back houses since at least 1881. Indeed William the elder was a true Summer Laner.

In 1861 and aged five, he had been living with his mother, Harriett, and three older siblings in a back house in Court 20. Harriet was the head of the household. A widow, she was 46 and worked as a dressmaker. Her oldest son, Henry, was twenty and was employed in a provision dealer's (grocery shop); her daughter, Esther, who was eighteen was a press worker; whilst Martha, who was nine, was a sewing machine worker.

William continued to live in and around The Lane all his life. In 1891, the Census recorded that the Kimber family was at number 2 house in 57, Court, Summer Lane. Ten years later they had moved nearby to Tower Street and by 1911 the Kimbers had managed to move up a little in the social pecking order by renting a front house at 100 Hospital Street. They stayed there until William's death in 1935 aged 80.

As for his wife, Catherine, she was the daughter of Martin and Maria Farrell. Her father was a bricklayer's labourer and both her parents had been born in Ireland. According to the 1871 Census, the Farrells lived in Mary Anne Street, a short street that went on from St Paul's Square, it ran into Henrietta Street. This ended at Constitution Hill, across from which began Summer Lane — where the Kimbers lived.

Catherine was an electro-plater. Aged seventeen she had been born in Birmingham as had her younger sister, two nieces who lived with them, and her older sister Matilda, who was 21. Her age suggests that the Farrells had come to Birmingham during the terrible years of the famine, when hunger and death ravaged Ireland and forced so many of its people into exile. Although there were other Irish families there, Mary Anne Street was overwhelmingly English.

Writing about the Irish in Britain in 1891, the well-informed John Denvir was of the firm opinion that there were few places where the Irish were more intermixed and intermarried into the general population than in Birmingham. Catherine Farrell exemplifies his point. A second generation Irish Brummie, she worked like so many of her fellows at what had once been regarded as "an English trade" in a factory and she married an Englishman. Indeed the wedding of Catherine and William Kimber took place in November 1875 at St Philip's, which was a Church of England place of worship and not a Roman Catholic one. Both of them made their marks, indicating that they could not write.

By 1891, Catherine's children were Harry aged eleven, William nine, Joseph six, and Alfred five. They had a baby sister, Ann, who was three months old. Their father was now working as a brass caster and their mother was a laundress. Of course, the 1890s was

62

a decade when Birmingham was troubled by the peaky blinder and slogging gangs, notorious for their affrays and serious assaults. Billy Kimber was a teenager in those years, but whether or not he was in such a gang, he must have been gaining a reputation for violence because in 1901, and as a nineteen-year-old, he was in Winson Green Prison serving time for wounding.

His occupation was given as a brass caster, but soon after coming out of prison he was sentenced to two months' hard labour for assaulting two police constables. The *Birmingham Daily Mail* of August 28, 1901 recounted how he had hit one with a violent blow, causing a cut lip, and then acted in a violent manner at the police station. Kimber's oldest child, Maude Elizabeth, had been born a month earlier and a year later he married her mother, Maude Beatrice Harbidge. Ten years before and aged eight, Maude had been living in Ledsam Street in Ladywood with her older brother and three younger siblings and their mother and father, who was a painter. It is not known how she met Billy Kimber, but her great granddaughter, Juliet Banyard, was told that "Maude had a lovely singing voice and earned money singing in the pubs in Brum".

Juliet's grandmother was Kimber's second child, Annie, who was born in December 1903. There was another daughter, Jessica, but sadly she died a year after her birth in 1907. Juliet explains that her mom, Sheila, who was Annie's only child, said that "Annie was Billy's favourite. He was not much bothered with Maudie and she didn't care for him either. Maudie used to say, 'you owed our dad money, you paid with your life'."

Soon after little Jessica's death, Kimber left his family. Juliet's brother, Justin Jones, writes that "at some point between 1908 and 1911, Billy and Maude separated and divorced. He went to live with a woman called Florence Brooks, who I think was a relation of Ellen Brooks who lived with another gang member, George 'Brummy' Sage." Abandoned as she was, Maude Kimber "went back to live with her parents in King Alfred's Place with her two children, my beloved aunty Maude who gave me sweets every week, and grandmother, Annie, whom I never met, unfortunately".

Maude Kimber's new home was at number 9. In 1911 her father, John, was 68 and her mother, Elizabeth, was 53. He was a plumber whilst his wife and daughter were press workers in the steel pen trade — which was dependent upon the nimble, fast and skilled fingers of women. It must have been tough for Maude with two young daughters to care for and with ageing parents. By 1920 the Electoral Registers show her living in a back-to-back in Charlotte Street on the edge of the Jewellery Quarter, between Newhall Street and the Parade and at the back of the old Science Museum.

It was a big yard with thirteen houses. She was registered there until 1925 but unhappily in the September of the next year she died aged just 43. Juliet states that "Mom once tried to find the grave of Maude. She thinks she went to Robin Hood, but the records showed she had a pauper's funeral and there was no grave. She's still mad about this, knowing Billy had money."

And Billy Kimber did have money; a lot of money. He gained it from becoming the most powerful gangster in England who ruled the racecourses of England with the Birmingham Gang and importantly, his London allies: the Elephant Boys led by the fearsome McDonalds of South London; and George "Brummy" Sage of the Camden Town mob in North London. That rule was challenged from 1920 in the south of England by Darby Sabini, who led a gang from around Clerkenwell in London. Kimber and his allies would fight might and main to keep hold of their lucrative criminal activities and a bloody "war" would break out.

But how did Kimber rise to such power from the back streets of Birmingham? After abandoning his family to poverty and hardships, it seems that he travelled the country doing what he did best — picking pockets at racecourses and other big sporting events where crowds gathered. As such he followed the criminal path of many Birmingham thieves from the 1870s.

In 1911, the Census recorded him as a single man aged 28 and boarding at a house in Salford. It is obvious by describing himself as unmarried that his desertion of his family was final in his mind. Kimber gave his occupation as a turf accountant — a euphemism for a bookmaker. In reality, he was now travelling the country as one of the Brummagem Boys.

This was not a firmly organised gang like that of a mafia family with a don, captains and soldiers. Rather it was a loose grouping of various small bunches of thieves and fighting men that could occasionally be brought together into a formidable force. Tall, sturdily built, and charismatic, according to those who knew him, Kimber was a member of one of those small gangs.

In January 1913, the *Derby Evening Telegraph* reported that on the 13th of that month a cup tie had been played in the city and that the local police had placed officers at the railway station to watch out for known criminals arriving by train. Amongst a group of eight men, they recognised William Kimber, his younger brother, Joseph, and a George White who were "expert travelling pickpockets and hotel thieves". The police followed them, but they were spotted by the Birmingham men who ran off, chased by the police "through several streets, for half or three-quarter of a mile, and both the Kimbers threw something out of their pockets into the snow".

The men made their escape down different entries to various houses. Only one of them was caught. He was George Ross, a tinsmith from Birmingham, who was charged with loitering with intent to commit a felony. The case against him was dismissed on the benefit of doubt. As for Kimber's brother, Joseph, the Birmingham Calendar of Prisoners highlight that he was a longstanding thief and they are a suggestive source for the criminality of Billy.

In July 1906 Joseph had been sentenced to six months' hard labour for stealing £7 from the person of Charles Edward Pearson whilst in Birmingham. Aged 21 and ostensibly a tailor, Joseph Kimber was already a hardened criminal. Four years before, in March 1902, he had been given a month in jail for stealing 24 shillings in Wednesbury. Like earlier Birmingham pickpockets, he soon widened his sphere of operations from the West Midlands and in December 1903 he was sentenced at Dover Police Court to three months for stealing money.

He was now using the alias of Joseph Williams. Within a few months of his release, he was sent to prison for two months for loitering in Birmingham. That was in June 1904, but in September he was quickly sent back to jail for stealing a purse and money. These terms of imprisonment did not dissuade Joseph Kimber from his life of crime. In May 1905 the Birkenhead Police Court gave him a two month' sentence for loitering, as did the Doncaster Police Court on September 15 of that year. This latter conviction coincided with the St Leger Festival at the Doncaster races and emphasised that he was a racecourse villain.

A year later, Joseph Kimber was arrested again under the assumed name of Joseph Williams. On January 29, 1906, the *Birmingham Daily Mail* reported that he was one of "a quartet of burly-built youths" charged with travelling from London to Birmingham on a Saturday without paying their fare and with altering the date on their ticket. He was given as a dealer living in Heaton Street, Hockley. The others were his brother, William Kimber, a caster of 40 Court, Brearley Street, in the Summer Lane neighbourhood; W. T. Eccles, a brass polisher of Great Russell Street; and William Taylor, a bookmaker's clerk of Vauxhall Grove. Each of them "bore bad reputations, and had been convicted for various offences at different times"; and each of them was fined a guinea with the alternative of a month in prison.

The *Derby Evening Telegraph* account of 1913 emphasises that Joseph and Billy Kimber continued to operate in the same gang of pickpockets but by now Billy Kimber had also palled up with a Londoner called George Sage. Some reports state that they had met in Winson Green Prison back in 1901, but what is certain is that the two men became friends and allies — so much so that even though he was from Stoke Newington, Hackney, Sage was nicknamed "Brummy".

It is also believed that the youthful Kimber was introduced to the racecourse rackets by the older Sage — although the long-lasting involvement of the Brummagem Boys in such criminality would seem to have been a more likely entry point for Kimber. However Sage could well have introduced Kimber to the southern racecourses around London. Certainly the ties between them were strengthened by 1921 because Kimber was then living with Florrie Brooks at 18, Warren Street, Islington and she was probably the sister of Ellen Brooks, the women with whom Sage lived.

He was also a fearless fist-to-fist fighter and gang leader. So too was another new friend of Kimber's: Wag McDonald from the *Elephant and Castle* in South London. His nephew, Brian McDonald has written an important and well-researched book called *Gangs of London* (Milo 2010). Unlike so many such works, it is neither sensationalised nor romanticised. Uniquely it is based on a compelling mixture of newspaper reports, legal evidence, personal observations, family stories and diaries, and photographs.

Brian explains that Wag was "a major south London gang leader, with a significant presence in the West End, where he was an early nightclub protector". By 1909 he had been joined by his younger brothers Wal, Jim, Bert and Tom, and he was controlling a number of illegal street betting pitches. Wag also hired himself as a "bodyguard" to racecourse bookmakers to protect them from gangs and obtained "favours" from other bookies.

It is likely that it was through these operations that he had met Kimber. The two men became firm friends. Brian's uncle Jim described Kimber "as a big, jovial well-liked fellow, respected as a settler of disagreements and disputes. He could fight and was a natural leader". Because of his friendship with the McDonalds it seems that whilst still maintaining his strong links with Birmingham, Kimber moved to London. Indeed Brian notes that "Kimber lived for a short while with my family at 116 York Road, Lambeth, before moving to Warren Street (now Grant Street), Islington".

In the summer of 1910, Kimber joined the McDonalds in fighting the McCausland brothers who were involved with Alf White's King's Cross Boys. The McDonalds gained the upper hand when Matt and Mike McCausland were jailed. In the aftermath, Kimber carried on thieving and pickpocketing across England, and it may be that he was also offering protection to bookmakers. However, he was now firmly based in London and not Birmingham, as was made plain by an intriguing article in the *Bedfordshire Advertiser and Luton Times* on April 17, 1914. It reported that "Dunstable's Bank Holiday was enlivened by a remarkable scene in the evening, a conflict between a party of Londoners returning from Towcester race meeting and the police".

The defendants included Anna Kimber aged 43, of the New Cut, Lambeth in South London, who was charged with being drunk and disorderly on the highway; and her husband, William, a china salesman aged 32, who had assaulted two policemen in the course of their duties. Who Anna was is a mystery. The other two defendants were Thomas Garnham (45), a china salesman from Upper Conduit Street, London, and his wife, Eliza (41), who were also both charged with obstructing one of the officers in his duty.

The 1911 census records a Thomas and Eliza Garnham living in Islington. Both had been born in Hoxton and both were dealers in china and glass, which they used to sell on the markets of North London. There was obviously a deep bond between Kimber and the Garnhams as on July 19, 1926 he would marry their daughter, Elizabeth, at Holborn Register Office in London. By then he was a widower aged 44 and she was 29.

All of the defendants pleaded guilty and expressed their regret for their behaviour to the magistrates. They had been returning from Towcester races by car and had stopped at several public houses on the way but did not eat. According to their counsel, "there was not the slightest doubt that they were the worse for wear for drink". He emphasised that this was their first appearance in a court of this kind — a blatant lie in the case of Billy Kimber.

The incident had begun when one of the policemen had heard Anna Kimber screaming and using the most filthy language. After she was arrested she continued to swear and kicked the officer several times, whilst at the station she shouted, "I will blow your — brains out when I get out. I shall know you again." On the way to the station, the officer was struck by William Kimber, who got on top in the ensuing struggle.

Kimber also struck the other constable in the side of the head. Fortunately for the Kimbers and Garnhams, the Bench took account of their guilty pleas and expressions of regret. Consequently, although it was recognised that these were very bad cases they did not take as severe view as they might have done. The defendants were fined a total of £8 6 shillings, which sum was paid by one of them.

By this time, Brian McDonald is of the opinion that Kimber had already taken control of the protection rackets on some major London racecourses. He believes that around 1910 a compromise was reached between race organisers and rogues, who were allowed to operate unfettered so long as they regulated themselves. As the Birmingham Gang was the strongest, the enforcement of this "regulation" fell to them led by Billy Kimber.

Certainly the problems of theft, pickpocketing and violence at many of the meetings around London especially had reached unacceptable levels. In August 1899 newspapers had carried reports on the arrest of James Gartell, the ringleader of the notorious Girdle Gang. Made up of 20–30 roughs it had recently attacked the racecourse police at Lingfield when the officers had apprehended a welsher. Three of them had been injured. According to the *Leeds Mercury*, the prosecution was brought by the racecourse authorities and the Jockey Club "who were determined to suppress injury to persons and riotous conduct at race meetings". They failed.

The *Lincolnshire Chronicle* reported on March 27, 1903 that a Joseph MacDonald had been charged with attempted pickpocketing at the Lincoln Races. A detective sergeant explained to the court that the accused was covered by three confederates but that after a time they stopped trying to pick pockets. MacDonald then took a hook out of his own pocket and "commenced going round to the bookmakers demanding rent". The other three men supported him in his demands and if a bookie refused to give them anything "they threatened to knock off his head". Indeed, MacDonald was so sure of his own fighting prowess that he had taken his jacket off to fight the detective.

He and his fellows were racecourse thieves "who went round to bookmakers demanding rent, which they had no business and no power to do". This assertion was supported by detectives from Birmingham and Nottingham. Like Billy Kimber and other gang leaders, MacDonald was not only a hard man but also he was an intelligent man. He cross-examined the detectives himself, which "gave rise to considerable amusement". It was evident he had no high opinion of the officers and "he told them bluntly that there would never be a Sherlock Holmes amongst them". MacDonald was sentenced to a month in jail.

Unhappily the detective sergeant's declaration that men like MacDonald had no power to demand rent from bookies was wrong. They had the power of fear gained from the power of physical bullying itself gained from the power of violence and numbers. This was exemplified by an account in the *Manchester Courier and Lancashire General Advertiser* of July 14, 1908 which revealed that a police officer at Haydock Races was set upon when he seized a man called Flint whom he saw steal a purse from a racegoer's pocket. Flint was amongst a group in the silver rings whose movements were suspicious. His fellows tried to release him and the policeman was badly mauled until assistance came to him.

The same year, on October 21, the *Nottingham Evening Post* stated that a gang of racing thieves had been operating at Newmarket. Two of them were William White and Frank Lester, who were sentenced to three months' imprisonment on a charge of being suspected persons unlawfully frequenting the refreshment rooms of the town's station with intent to commit a felony. White had 27 previous convictions against his name.

A more "remarkable outrage" was perpetrated after the Windsor Races in early June 1910. According to the

Western Times a gang of about 40 thieves boarded various launches taking people back from the races and "after threatening to throw the captains overboard if they interfered proceeded to rob the passengers of all their valuables". They then got clear away when the launches stopped at Windsor.

Given such appalling events it would not be surprising if some managements had approached Billy Kimber to take control of their racecourses. Crucially, he had strong backup from two feared London gangs: the Elephant Boys from south of the River Thames, under the leadership of his friends the McDonald brothers; and the Camden Town mob from North London, led by another pal, George "Brummy" Sage.

But in the late summer of 1914 Kimber, the McDonalds, Sage and others like them lost their main sources of income when the First World War broke out. All horse racing was ended, except for Newmarket's July Course. Kimber joined up, but was either discharged or had deserted by 1915. Once peace came and racecourses re-opened, he returned to his old ways, and for a short time, he rose to become the most powerful gangster in England. That position brought him and his allies into conflict with the Sabini Gang of Clerkenwell in London and their allies.

CHAPTER
FIVE

Racecourse War

In the early twentieth century, many parts of English racecourses were unruly places. Megging mobs fleeced all and sundry with the "three-card trick"; whilst gangs of pickpockets and thieves preyed upon spectators, beating up any who retaliated. One of the most notorious was the Aldgate Mob. According to Sam Dell, a respected London bookmaker, their leader was "a right villain" and "they used to operate mostly on bank holidays and high days. They'd be twenty-handed and they would lift a guy in the air and someone would take his money."

Bookies were also victimised. They had "to arrive early in the morning to stake a claim for their pitch and be prepared to be blackmailed or prepared to fight the local gang. You had to be prepared to bung or be prepared to fight." In these circumstances some bookmakers hired boxers to act as minders and one leading layer from Birmingham paid the famed Owen Moran to look out for him. A Summer Laner, it was said that Moran's mother could "wipe the floor with any two ordinary men", whilst his sister, Annie, was a noted fighting woman. Owen himself was a fearless boxer and would take on anyone — and he fought in America where he gained a fearsome reputation as the best pound for pound fighter in the world.

Even the toughest of gangsters avoided Owen Moran, but most bookmakers could not afford to pay for such protection. A favourite dodge of these gangs was to go round with a bogus subscription for "poor old Bill", and "dear old Charlie" who had hit hard times — or for a fatherless family on the brink of starvation. Those who did not pay up were marked men and often had a bad time of it. Another ruse was to shout out a bet to a bookie. If the horse the gang had backed won they would expect to be paid out, if it lost they held on to their money.

With the end of the First World War, racing resumed and as with other sports, attendances soared in the post-war boom. They peaked in 1919 and 1920 but thereafter still remained much more than before 1914, although they then dropped significantly from 1925 as the staple industries declined and the British economy struggled. Much higher attendances were matched by much higher spending on betting as emphasised by the story of Bud Flanagan, who later became a bookie, as told in the *Centenary Supplement* of the *Sporting Chronicle* of May 29, 1971. In 1919 his bets on four races at Ayr "disposed of the whole of his gratuity earned in three-and-a-half-years of soldiering".

Such outlays meant profitable plundering. These drew in not only gangs specialising in pickpocketing, like that from Aldgate, but also the gangs from London and Birmingham who had run the protection rackets before the war. And with the prospects of making big sums of money some of the gangsters from the Midlands were pulled to live in the capital, which was well connected by railway to all parts of the country and was central to some of the most popular meetings in the land.

On May 16, 1919, *The Manchester Guardian* noted that the Chester magistrates had sentenced Albert Gilliard and Richard Ronan to three months' imprisonment for stealing a wallet with £11 in it. Inspector Whitehouse from Birmingham described the men as belonging to a gang of about eight Birmingham men who were working in Chester during the races. He added that they were at Birmingham for a few years but had migrated to London, whence they worked different districts.

Two months later, on June 24, *The Times* recounted how three men had demanded money from book-makers at Ascot. Several paid up without demur. Then one of the men called William MacNamara said to another bookie, "give us a pound or you will go up in the air". The layer refused, whereupon he was knocked off his box by Patrick Daily whilst his satchel filled with money was grabbed at by MacNamara.

Quickly such organised gangs began to draw attention. On October 18, 1919, the *Daily Mail* carried a report on "Racecourse Gangs", asserting that "racecourse robberies with violence were said to be increasing". A few months later, on January 22, 1920, *The Times* regretted that gangsterism was on the rise and that as well as old hands they included younger men who were ex-soldiers. Service in the Army had taught them the value of organisation, whilst "their training in discipline has accustomed them to higher minds, and there seems little doubt that superior intelligence is at work in the direction and carrying out of larger crimes".

Although not aimed specifically at the racecourse gangs, these acute observations were most appropriate to them. Then national attention was drawn to "disgraceful scenes" at Salisbury Races in early July 1920. Visitors to the course were held up and robbed of all they possessed with violence and impunity; whilst roughs forced drivers of cars to take them to the railway station and treated them with brutality if they refused.

A special correspondent to the *Yorkshire Post and Leeds Intelligencer* pronounced on July 10 that it was the most disgraceful meeting that he had ever attended. The local police paid by the racecourse management to keep order had acted "magnificently" but "they had work to do which they ought not to have been asked to do". When told by a Salisbury steward that he believed that the Jockey Club should set up a permanent force of racecourse police to keep order, the correspondent replied that "the only way to deal with the class of desperadoes who look on Salisbury Races as a beanfeast is to deal with them before they enter the city".

This meant that they should be stopped at both Waterloo Station and Birmingham — and if they got past then they should be stopped at Salisbury railway station. The rejoinder by the steward highlighted the futility of such an approach: "they would easily circumvent that by char-a-bancs". The steward was right. Just as the expansion of the railway network had enabled organised gangs of roughs to travel further afield from their bases, so too now would motorised transport facilitate the passage of gangs across the country — and it would do so more secretly.

The shocking events at Salisbury prompted *The Times* to call for immediate action against "rogues of the racecourse". On July 17, 1920 a major article deplored "the rowdyism and robbery which, since the war, have been going on to an ever-increasing extent at practically all the race meetings up and down the country". The roughs responsible worked in organised gangs and they were "undoubtedly capitalised. How else can they afford to travel in luxurious motor-cars to meetings as far away from London as Newmarket, Gatwick and Lingfield."

Moreover their organisation was emphasised by the way that they covered each other enabling "the worker of the more desperate assaults to escape. Outwardly they do not know each other on such occasions but they are at other times seen together and most certainly share all the spoils". At the recent Ascot meeting great numbers of people had sustained losses from thieves and pickpockets, and now it was feared that the criminals would descend upon the Goodwood meeting.

Appallingly, not only were racegoers robbed and defrauded but also private cars were held up on the highway and their drivers forced by threats and insults, to drive the hijackers to a race meeting. In this way they avoided the police who were watching for their movement by train; and indeed the local police were unable to cope as they did not know the ruffians and nor could they spare the resources.

This hooliganism was "very lucrative" — and it was the easy wealth to be gained from such criminality that drew in new gangs which sought to muscle in on what had been the preserves of the Birmingham Gang and its London allies. On August 23, 1920 *The Times* explained that five men had been arrested at the Hurst Park meeting for obtaining money by threats and picking pockets. Detective Inspector Grosse of Scotland Yard stated that they were "members of an organised gang who frequented the outside of racecourses and railways".

Each was found guilty and sentenced to between a month and three months' imprisonment with hard labour. As Brian McDonald has shown, they were members of Alf White's King's Cross Boys and Dodger Mullins' Bethnal Green Gang. Soon after this case, the two gangs fell out and they fought a bloody battle at Brighton. At another meeting there in the summer of 1920, some of the Sabini Gang went round the outside part of the course, which was free to enter.

Brian McDonald writes that led by Joe Sabini they forced bookies, punters and rogues alike to throw half-crowns into a bucket for their "services". Those who refused were forced off and one reluctant bookmaker was cut with a razor. Kimber had a "token force" there and they were run off. However when the Sabinis returned to try their tricks again, they were met by a large force led by Wal McDonald. Aggrieved bookmakers had contacted Kimber who sent his trusted ally to sort out the usurping gang. And he did. The Sabinis were frisked and their collection money was confiscated, and then all of them "were given a kicking as a disincentive to be so cheeky in future". It was a humiliation for Joe Sabini and as a result a humiliation for his brother, Darby.

Brian McDonald feels that the racecourse managements were fearful that neither they nor the police could counter the new gangs and so they also turned to Kimber to restore order. Because the Birmingham Gang was the strongest, the enforcement of this "regulation" fell to them led by Billy Kimber.

As Brian comments, in the immediate post-war period the Birmingham Gang and their London allies "expelled Mullins' gang from the courses and Kimber used his new alliances to move into the London underworld". Kimber's ability to extend the reach of the Birmingham Gang from the meetings in the Midlands and the North to the more lucrative racecourses in the South was also aided by the "tacit understanding" of the police officers who were engaged to keep the peace at race meetings.

In his *Sunday Mercury* article of January 1935, Fairfax-Blakeborough explained that an ex-detective had told him that when he had first joined the force the same officers from all over the country were employed by particular managements on race days. This was because "they were supposed to know all the Birmingham gang and the 'boys' from London, Leeds and elsewhere". The former policeman went on to state that a colleague was one of these officers and that on his first assignment he had been shown around Doncaster Races by an "old hand" who had been so instructed by a senior inspector.

The newcomer was told that "we always make a bit for ourselves here, you know". He replied that as a stranger he was there to do as he was told. Having given the right response he was taken back to the inspector with the report that "everything will be alright". At the end of four days' racing the young officer was handed £50 as his share of the proceeds, "which could not have been anything but the bribes of those who paid for non-interference, for the £50 was altogether from his pay". If a young constable received such a large sum then "how much did others of higher rank get to shut their eyes to the doings of the gang? I believe one racecourse detective died worth £22,000."

The key figure in organising the protection rackets effectively was Billy Kimber — and he would also have some control over the pickpockets, thieves and other tricksters who swarmed upon the racecourses. For at least the previous twenty years he had led a life of crime, having started out in a small gang of Birmingham pickpockets and thieves operating at sporting events. There were a number of other such gangs from the city and Kimber went on to bring them together into a frightening force of violent men known as the Birmingham Gang. The leader of such a fearsome bunch had to be a hard man himself. And Kimber was hard.

Tall, well-built and strong, he was remembered by the late Denny Green, a well-respected bookie, as "a game un', he was a fearless fighter and he fought fairly with his hands and didn't use knives". Denny recalled that on one occasion during the First World War, Kimber was in Dublin and was attacked by a group of men when he was on a bridge over the River Liffey. Single-handedly he fought them off.

But Kimber was more than a hard man. Others amongst the Birmingham Gang were notorious for their vicious and bloody crimes yet it was Kimber who became their leader — albeit a leader of a loose and unstable grouping. He must have done so not only through his physical power but also through his organisational skills and the force of his personality.

Tom Divall was a former chief inspector at Scotland Yard who was employed by the racecourses to keep order at various meetings and he recognised Kimber as a charismatic figure. In 1919 Divall was in charge of one of the rings of spectators at Doncaster. There was a large crowd and a dangerous situation arose over a disputed bet. The course officials and police lost control as "high words and ugly threats passed between some miners and bookmakers' runners". Divall feared "an awful scrimmage" and then "up came Billy Kimber, a host in himself among his fellows, and he soon settled the disturbance".

Divall was certain that Kimber was "one of the best" and the Birmingham man was also respected by some London racecourse bookmakers even though he made his money by providing "services" for them and protecting them. Ali Harris was a leading southern racecourse bookie and he praised Kimber as a "pretty well respected bloke".

Although he later described himself as a bookmaker from Bordesley, in reality Kimber was not. Instead, he controlled the most prominent five or six pitches at each meeting which took the most money in bets. He put on them either his own men or bookmakers for a return of "ten bob in the pound" — 50% of the profit.

But that was not the end of the scams for making money, because Kimber, McDonald and Sage had to make big sums of cash not only for themselves but also for their men. As Sam Dell stressed "to be a successful gangster they had to have money coming in to pay their hirelings see. You had to have plenty of money coming in to keep a team together. Once they couldn't keep the team together well that was the end of the gang."

Kimber made that money and kept his team together with the help of one of the key figures in the Birmingham Gang, a man called Andrew Towie (or Towey). He may have been helped by a brother as Lou Price, another London bookmaker, remembered that a Jack Towie was one of the hard men of the Birmingham Gang. Be that as it may, Andrew Towie is a mysterious figure.

Like Kimber, he relocated to the south to be closer to the busiest racecourses and lived in Kingston. Towie was remembered by Charles Maskey, a well-known racing man from the capital, as "a good man"; whilst Sam Dell declared that Towie was "a man of great respect, and so was Kimber respected". Towie himself "was a tremendous gambler. In those days he'd have a monkey (£500) on a horse and he used to sit there on a stool, I can see him now, and they'd come and give him information about the prices and he'd send them away to have a bet. But he was the one they all looked up to in Birmingham, and of course Billy Kimber."

It seems that Towie's family came from Nottingham but settled in Birmingham when he was a boy. Whatever the case, Towie either came up with or developed the idea of selling dots and dashes cards for each race. This was a simple operation whereby each horse was pricked with symbols to alert bookies to its form and to its chances in the race. In fact, this "service" told the layer nothing more than he knew already and it was merely a means to obtain money from him.

Then there was the calling out the numbers of the horses in a particular race, while bookmakers were "encouraged" to pay for "tools of the trade". Included among these were pieces of chalk with which to mark up the prices of the horses on their boards; water and sponges with which to rub them out; and stools on which to stand.

Sam Dell recalls that "it was the Birmingham mob that used to run the stools at Cheltenham and places like that. And they used to have to cart the stools from track to track and they used to have a big van to do it in. And then when they got there, they were collapsible stools, used to have to bang the legs in, and they used to have to set all the stools up." Exorbitant prices could be charged as if a bookie did not have a stool to stand on then he was at a disadvantage to others.

Bookies usually paid 2s 6d (12.5p) for each "facility" and this added up to a lot of money. At a big meeting like Doncaster there could be more than 100 bookmakers each paying 2s 6d for each service per race and over six or more races. That could mean something like £300 to £400, or more, per meeting — although the sum was a lot less at smaller events. To that could be added the "genuine" protection money, and the cuts taken by the gangs from bookmakers' winnings.

Providing bookmakers with lists of runners for each race was particularly lucrative. Before 1914, rogues sold supposedly "official" race cards detailing the runners and riders for the day's racing at between 2d and 6d each, as indicated in a report on several arrests made at the local races in the *Leamington Spa Courier* on September 18, 1903. Of course they were not official but after the First World War the price for lists of runners and riders for each race rose considerably.

In January 1923 a court case took place relating to a shooting by the Cortesi brothers who had attacked Darby and Harry "Boy" Sabini at an Italian club in Clerkenwell. Formerly allies, they had come to blows over the money to be gained from racecourse rackets. On January 16, the *Western Daily Press* included Darby Sabini's responses as a witness in the trial at the Old Bailey. He told Lord Justice Darling that each list was sold for five shillings (25p) and that between £3,000 and £4,000 a year could be earned from them, with "sometimes as much £100, £200 a day".

Overall the profits were so great from all the rackets that in the 1930s the son of a leading Sabini Gang member from London recalled that his father would come home from the races with bags full of silver. So much was there, that the coins were poured into the bath — whence they were shared out with his father's associates.

Kimber, Towie, McDonald, and Sage would obviously take their cuts from the rackets and allowing for twenty gangsters at a big meeting that would mean that each of the gang member could earn perhaps £15–£20 or more a day for not working. And that was without the money brought in from the picking of pockets and thefts. This was a tremendous amount of money in 1920, when a skilled man would be lucky to earn £4.50p for a week's hard collar, whilst a labourer would be paid no more than £2 weekly for real work. As for each of the gang leaders, from their share of the rackets and control of the best pitches each of them could be bringing in huge sums, well upwards of £100 per day.

A fighting man with magnetism, Kimber was indeed the kind of person of "superior intelligence" as described in *The Times* article on gang leaders — and he brought direction and organisation to the racecourse rackets. But such easy money aroused covetous eyes, amongst them those of Edward Emanuel. Little is known about his early life but he came to notice in 1904 when he threatened to shoot an Islington street trader and was charged with possession of a loaded revolver. Emanuel stated he was a salesman but the magistrate declared that he was "a dangerous fellow" and imposed a high surety of £250 or twelve months' imprisonment.

Four years later, a John McCarthy attempted to kill Emanuel in East London. Both men were described as market porters. Over the next few years Emanuel established himself as a proprietor of spielers (illegal gambling clubs), a fixer of boxing fights, and a controller of illegal off-course betting pitches. It was also alleged that he had some police officers "in his pocket" and that for a payment he could arrange lighter sentences for Jewish criminals. Arthur Harding's criminal life has been detailed by Raphael Samuel in *East End Underworld* (1981) and well-informed as he was, Harding was certain that by the early 1920s, Emanuel was regarded "as in charge of the whole East End underworld — or at least the Jewish part of it".

Emanuel's opportunity to take over Kimber's rackets and legitimate business of the printing of racing lists came in 1921. Jewish bookies from the East End were being terrorised by three South Londoners associated with Kimber. Divall declaimed them as "low blackguards, always more or less full of liquor". Known as the "Lunies", they were joined by some Brummies and they were blackmailing the Jewish bookies on top of the payments they were already making to Kimber for his "services".

One of the Jewish bookies beaten up badly by them was Alfie Solomon, the leader of a gang of Jewish toughs. A violent man himself, he would be a key figure in the "war" that would soon break out. Solomon's brother betted under the name of Sydney Lewis, and he explained to me in the late 1980s that it became "us against them, the North against the South". There is no doubt that the attacks on the Jewish bookies were fuelled by racism as much as by greed, for as Simmy Lewis stated "if I'd put up as Simmy Solomon as a bookie I wouldn't take a penny".

Born in 1901, Lou Prince was an East End racecourse bookie with a Jewish father. He respected Andrew Towie but also saw the Birmingham team "take liberties". He remembered that the Jewish bookies turned to Emanuel for help because he was "a financial power" and "the guvnor before Darby Sabini". Because Emanuel was "pally with the Italian push", he brought in Sabini and his gang to provide protection for the Jewish bookies.

Ottavio "Darby" Sabini grew up in London's Little Italy in Clerkenwell, having an English mother, Eliza Handley, who was born in Holborn. His Italian father was also called Ottavio and in 1888 he was imprisoned for wounding — and he would go on to be involved in more violence. Twelve years later, the younger Sabini was in an industrial school, a place for "disorderly children". When he married Annie Emma Potter in 1913 at St Philip's Clerkenwell, an Anglican Church, Darby gave his occupation as a carman but it was not one that he followed.

His nickname of Darby is thought to have come from the fact that he was a south paw boxer — and that name was given to all such. Smaller than Kimber at 5 foot 8, Sabini was stocky, solid, and hard-hitting, although his punches were often strengthened with a knuckle duster, whilst he was also known to carry a gun. By the end of the First World War, Sabini was the "guvnor" of a gang from around Clerkenwell in London that included his brothers, of whom Harry "Boy" and Joe were the most prominent.

Despite the wealth he gained from his criminality, in his heyday Darby Sabini was unostentatious. He wore a flat cap, collarless shirt, high-buttoned waistcoat, and dark suit. Billy Hill, a later gangland boss stated that Sabini "stood for no liberties", while bookie Lou Prince remembered that "he was the gentleman of the mob but he feared no one". In his memoirs in 1960, former chief superintendent Edward Greeno underlined the fearful aspect of the gang from Little Italy, for Sabini and "his thugs used to stand sideways on to let the bookmakers see the hammers in their pockets".

Like him, some of his gang were of Italian descent, although others were not. Moreover, Darby allied with Alfie Solomon's Jewish tearaways and the King's Cross Gang of Big Alf White. They soon began to make their moves. Backed up by this "muscle", it seems that the Jewish bookies refused to pay protection to the Birmingham Gang at the Sandown Park Military Meeting on March 12, 1921. One of them was a Jewish bookmaker called Lewis. Of course, Sydney Lewis was the bookmaking name of Alfie Solomon's youngest brother and in this instance it appears that it was actually Alfie Solomon himself who was taking the bets — as suggested by Greeno in his book. In his book *Everybody Boo* (1951) boxing referee Moss Deyong graphically described what happened to Solomon after his refusal "to bung".

Suddenly the mobster swung his race-glasses, heavy and solid, into the bookmaker's face. Down went Lewis, and the assailant promptly stepped on his unprotected face as he lay on the ground, immediately afterwards slipping away into the crowd. Lewis was picked up, his face a bloody mass and with several teeth missing. From that moment the gang wars between the North and South opened up in earnest.

Tragically, another Jewish bookmaker was killed. Philip Jacobs, also known as Oker, was aged 53 and from Whitechapel. According to *The Times* of August 2, his widow told the inquest that he had returned home from the meeting with his head bandaged because he had been hit on the head with a hammer. He was never the same man again and at the end of July, after attending Goodwood races, he had been taken to hospital where he died.

Samuel Hirschowitz was a friend of Mr Jacobs and had been with him at Sandown along with his own brother-in-law, Abraham Joel. He reported that he saw a man called Armstrong striking Joel. The two closed and the witness, trying to separate them, was struck by Armstrong who forced him to the ground "and kicked him for all he was worth". There were plenty of people about but they were all afraid of Armstrong. Mr Jacobs went to help his friend but was hit on the head by

Armstrong. Mrs Jacobs then told the inquest that "everybody knows Armstrong. He is a big and desperate man". So he was.

Aged 47, Thomas Samuel John Armstrong of Conybere Street in Highgate described himself as a bookmaker but in reality he was one of Kimber's hard men. The coroner gave the cause of Mr Jacobs' death as meningitis accelerated by the blow to his head and Armstrong was charged with manslaughter. He appeared at the Old Bailey on September 9, and it would appear that the intimidation of witnesses played a crucial role in the trial. As reported in the *Derby Evening Telegraph*, one of those who gave evidence against Armstrong was a bookmaker called Maurice Forman.

He told the court that he seen Armstrong hit Jacobs on the head with a pair of field glasses. Later the Birmingham man had come up to him and demanded money. Forman gave him £2 "because there were four or five men with him and I was afraid of my life". The defence counsel pointed out that at the inquest Forman had said that he had not seen anything in Armstrong's arms. Forman replied that he was "threatened outside the coroner's court with my life if I spoke the truth. I have asked for police protection". Armstrong denied that he had struck Jacobs and he was found not guilty.

On the same day as the Sandown Park meeting, Billy and Joe Kimber attacked a member of the Mullins Gang and were bound over to keep the peace. Less than two weeks afterwards, Darby Sabini was charged with shooting at persons unknown at Greenford Park

Trotting Track. The incident was widely reported in detail, as in the *Dundee Courier* of March 21. Inspector Heaps told Ealing Police Court that he had heard shouting and saw Sabini facing a crowd of men. There were cries of "Shoot the —". Then "there was a shot and smoke arose above Sabini's head. He had a revolver in his hand."

The inspector ran to the right side of Sabini and ordered him to stop but the crowd was trying to rush him and he was shouting, "I'll shoot". A police sergeant came and threw his arms around Sabini, but "men struck at him with pieces of wood and with bottles. One man had a piece of wood and was shouting, 'I'll murder him'." There was a struggle to get the revolver from Sabini and when that was achieved he was taken to Greenford Police station for his protection. When he was charged he explained that he had been given the revolver that day "as I looked like getting murdered . . . About 20 of those Birmingham racecourse pests got hold of me".

As it turned out, the revolver only had blank cartridges although Sabini was found to have a cut-throat razor on him. The charge of shooting against him was dismissed but he was fined £10 for being in possession of a gun without a licence. It is suspected that Sabini had paid the police to help him. Two of the men who had led the attack on him were Sandy Rice and Frederick Gilbert. They had been charged with disturbing the peace but that was also dismissed. Rice was in reality Alex Tomaso, a man of Italian descent who sided against the Sabinis, whilst Gilbert was another London ally of Kimber.

Days later, according to Brian McDonald, Matt McCausland confronted his old enemy Kimber in the *Lord Nelson* in Cleveland Street, Marylebone: "perhaps he thought the Brummie, being from the sticks was an easy mark. But Kimber made a bloody example of McCausland". About the same time two Sabini men tried to force their way into Wag McDonald's home in Walworth. Both were knocked down and dragged to their car "as a message to Darby".

Then at the end of March, Kimber himself was shot. This attack would herald a year of escalating violence on the racecourses of England as Kimber's Birmingham Gang and his London allies fought with the Sabinis and their supporters for control of the ill-gotten wealth from protection rackets.

On March 29, 1921, the *Manchester Guardian* included the headline "Bookmaker Found Shot. Mysterious London Affair". This "bookmaker" was Billy Kimber. The newspaper reported that on the previous morning, Easter Monday, he had been lying in the roadway at Collier's Street in King's Cross, London. He had a bullet wound in one side and his head was badly cut. According to the *Dundee Courier*, Kimber had been shot in a nearby house where "a number of men well known in racing circles" had held a merry party, with drinking and singing until the early hours of the morning.

A neighbour recounted that about midnight there was a commotion outside and it looked as if about half a dozen men "were trying to eject one of the party, who protested vigorously and who succeeded in wrenching himself free and getting back in the house". That man was Alfie Solomon, the Jewish gangster and bookie who had been badly beaten up at Sandown and was allied with the Sabinis. It seems that their leader, Darby, had asked Kimber and his pal, Wag McDonald, to a meeting to discuss making peace. However, when Solomon arrived Kimber went for him and was shot.

Wag's nephew Brian McDonald writes that his uncle emphasised that "Kimber had a hatred for Solomon, who he saw was one of the scum that threatened racecourse bookies at the edge of a razor and whom he had driven from racecourses" and that Solomon wanted to "get back to the lucrative business of skinning bookies".

Kimber was taken to hospital. The bullet had gone through him and after recovering from heavy bleeding, he discharged himself. By then Solomon had gone to the police and stated that he had shot Kimber by accident. Solomon was charged with unlawful wounding but in the *Hull Daily Mail* of April 6, the prosecutor made it clear that the evidence was of the slenderest and that Kimber "now absolutely refuses to say anything about the affair". Because of this, the case was dismissed on April 27.

Kimber had given his address as Hospital Street, Birmingham, but it is likely that this was the home of his parents as he was now living with his girlfriend,

Florence Brooks, in Warner Street, Clerkenwell in London. Whatever the case, he was determined to put on a show of strength in the south of England. He did so on Saturday April 4 at Alexandra Park and because he was still recuperating from his wound, his men were led by his friend George "Brummy" Sage.

The *Sunday Post* exclaimed that a riot ensued; whilst the racing correspondent of *The Times* bemoaned "the disgraceful scenes" at the meeting caused by "a very large number of rogues, who live by blackmail and pocket-picking". Amongst these undesirables "there were many members of two organised gangs of ruffians — one lot from Birmingham and the other from London — who had a difference of opinion". Before racing began "these two gangs came to blows. They, of course, cannot fight cleanly so they used knives, life preservers — falsely called — and apparently pistols, for one man was taken away shot in the head".

Lou Prince was bookmaking there that day. He remembered that the ring "was packed and the Birmingham Mob went into Tattersall's in Indian file. Their leader had a shooter and when they went into the ring looking for the Italian mob everyone dispersed and ran for cover as soon as they saw the shooter."

In the aftermath, William Joyce said he had been assaulted with a hammer and was treated for severe cuts; whilst a Birmingham man, Anthony Martin, was charged with attempting to murder a Londoner called James Best. Martin was actually Antonio Martino who was an Italian Brummie living in Bridge Street West. Aged 42 he described himself as a professional backer of horses but he was in fact a major figure in the Birmingham Gang.

In court on July 4, the prosecutor asserted that just before the first race at Alexandra Park, Best was surrounded by a gang of men — one of whom shouted "That is one of them". Best tried to get away but was chased, hit on the head from behind and knocked down. Police Constable Hunter was nearby and he saw "Martin push his way through the crowd with a revolver in his hand, fire at Best, who lay on the ground, and then throw away the revolver".

However the gun that was recovered was rusty and had not been fired recently. Moreover, whoever had fired at Best had missed, for he was wounded with a blunt instrument and not by a shot. Best himself did not identify Martin "either because he could not or he would not". The Birmingham man pleaded not guilty, pronouncing that he was not a member of the Birmingham Gang. Described as a man of good character, the jury agreed with him.

By now the violence was escalating, and members of the two sides clashed by Mornington Crescent tube station on April 20. A shot was fired and it was said that one man wielded a bludgeon made out of a German hand grenade case tied to a short stick. Then on June 2, 1921 there took place what The Times declared was "The Epsom Road Battle".

According to Detective Inspector Stevens, after the Epsom races that day he received a telephone call at the local police station that a "Sinn Fein riot" was happening on the London Road in Ewell. When he arrived with his officers he found three men suffering from wounds and two badly-damaged motor cars. Information later came that the men who had caused the trouble were drinking at a pub in Kingston. A large force of police was sent there and 28 men from Birmingham were arrested.

It seems that at about 4.30p.m. that day they had pulled up in a motor tender and a taxi. One of the men kept scanning the road with field glasses. He was watched by a local householder who told the press that about an hour later he heard the man say, "Here they come boys". One of the cars was then run full speed up the hill and collided with an oncoming charabanc: "both the tyres of the Birmingham car burst with loud reports and the gang of ten or fifteen men attacked the occupants of the other car with hammers, hatchets, bottles, bricks and hedge sticks".

Six of the victims were taken to hospital with scalp wounds. They and the others on the charabanc were bookmakers from Leeds, most of whom were Jewish. Previously they had been regarded as supporters of Kimber but they were attacked because it was believed that they were switching sides to the Sabinis. The prisoners appeared in court in Epsom on June 4. *The Times* noted that they had been due to be moved there from Kingston Police Station at about noon, by which time a large crowd of up to 1500 people had gathered. However, officers from Scotland Yard's Flying Squad advised the local police to split up the Birmingham men and the crowd had dispersed by the time that seven motor fenders arrived from London.

The prisoners were handcuffed "but wore a careless air, many smoking cigarettes as they drove away". They were escorted by 40 policemen, many of whom were armed. These included the motorcyclists who led the column. The 28 men were brought to trial on July 19, charged with conspiring to cause grievous bodily harm to ten men from Leeds and with conspiring with persons unknown to cause unlawful and malicious wounding. All bar one were also charged with being in possession of arms and ammunition.

Over the next few days six men were discharged. They were Percy Milner, a coster aged 32; Thomas Manders, a rubber worker, 34; Thomas Riley, a capstan hand, 30; Michael Galvin, an asphalter, 41; Joseph Wilson, a miner, 45; and William Giles, the taxi driver, 28. Then on July 23 another five were found not guilty: Charles Roberts, a hawker, 41; Thomas Kingston, a machinist, 34; Abraham Whitehouse, a baker, 22; George Davies, a millwright, 28; and William Graham, a fruiterer aged 42. Known as Cockney Bill, Graham had been given a five-year sentence for wounding in 1912. He was now living with Annie Moran, the sister of the famed Birmingham boxer, Owen Moran, and a fighting woman herself.

A large number of police officers were in the court at Guildford Assizes as the verdicts on the final day were read. They were there to prevent a demonstration by the crowd of racing men in the gallery. The judge pronounced sentence first on 32-year-old Arthur Vincent, a bookmaker. Because he had no previous convictions and a good Army record he was sentenced to nine months' hard labour. Thomas Conway, a labourer aged 36 also had a good character and received the same sentence. So too did Ernest Hughes, a coster, 28; William Goulding, a labourer, 45; and Thomas Tuckey, a wire worker, 33.

William Hayden, a 38-year-old butcher had been made to work down German mines as a prisoner of war. He had "one or two" other convictions and was given ten months' hard labour. Sentences of twelve months' hard labour were handed to William Bayliss, a labourer aged 47 and to William O'Brien, a capstan hand, 29; whilst Thomas Eivers, a polisher, 29, was committed to fourteen months' hard labour.

Several other convictions were proved against Alfred Thomas, a 30-year-old costermonger. After he was also given fourteen months' hard labour, he shouted "that is a miscarriage of justice!" Edward Banks a 43-year-old greengrocer and Edward Tuckey a bricklayer aged 34 were each sentenced to fifteen months' hard labour. Tuckey had been given the same term in 1906 for stealing a bicycle. His brother, Henry, was 38 and a bricklayer and was now handed eighteen months' hard labour.

The remainder of those convicted included some hardened criminals. Harry Stringer was a 32-year-old platelayer. He had eighteen previous convictions and was also sentenced to eighteen months' hard labour. So too was John Allard, aged 52 and a painter. Nine years before, Allard had stated he was a plumber when he had been sent down for seven years for the manslaughter of Charles Cutler in March 1911. Cutler, a hard man from Sparkbrook, had quarrelled with Allard, who had threatened to bodge out Cutler's eyes.

Armed with a knuckleduster, Cutler offered to fight Allard and one of his mates. Allard walked away but later, and in the dark, he attacked Cutler. Taken by surprise, Cutler fell to the ground, whereon Allard continued to punch him. He then picked up his umbrella and thrust its tip into the right eye of Cutler, who died the next day.

Brave passers-by restrained Allard but in court he was vouched for by witnesses, whilst he stated that Cutler had been the aggressor and that he had merely tried to hold him back with his umbrella. The jury was taken in by Allard and convicted him of manslaughter. His previous convictions were then read. He had eleven for assault, and one each for housebreaking, obstructing the police, loitering with intent and frequenting.

The final two convicted men were Joseph Witton, an agent aged 34, and John Lee, a 40-year-old bookmaker. Each of them was sentenced to three years' hard labour. On July 25, 1921 *The Times* reported that the police described Witton as "a violent, vicious and dangerous man". So he was. Between 1900 and 1907, Witton had received five convictions for theft; four for drunkenness; two for assault; and one each for drunk and disorderly, loitering and indecent language. Then in 1908 he was handed a four-year term in prison and a flogging for robbery with violence.

Like Stringer, Witton had served in the Worcestershire Regiment during the First World War and had been posted to France and Gallipoli. He had deserted twice

101

and was discharged from the Army when he was convicted for shop breaking in Birmingham in 1918. Stringer had also seen action in France, but had deserted three times and had also been discharged after a conviction.

As for the last of the Birmingham Gang to be sent down, John Lee was on ticket-of-leave from prison having been sentenced at Leeds five years before for unlawfully and maliciously wounding a woman called Ada Bailey. Like Witton and Allard, he was a most nasty man. In 1903 he had been imprisoned for three years for wounding and attempted murder; whilst in 1899 he had been sentenced to eighteen months for manslaughter. Lee had other convictions for theft and assault. When he heard his term, he remarked "thank you" and left the dock with a loud laugh.

Three other members of the Birmingham Gang were also jailed in a separate case for demanding money from bookmakers with threats at the Epsom Meeting. The *Daily Mail* of June 6, 1921 named them as Ernest Mack, a dealer aged 56; William Darby, a haulier, 39; and Charles Franklin, a metal worker, 41. They were accompanied by a man from Southampton.

A police witnesses stated that he saw them going through lines of bookmakers at Epsom, "stopping in front of each, and pushing through the crowd up to them. Invariably Darby put out his hand, and Franklin followed that up by saying, 'Give us £1, come on'." In most cases the bookmakers handed over some silver, but if any demurred then "the men assumed a threatening attitude, and Darby said, 'come on we are four-handed'". A threat was also made to knock over a bookmaker's joint. They made a lot of money from their bullying as they had intimidated 50 bookmakers.

For their offences, Darby was fined £25; whilst a term of three months in prison each was handed to Mack and Franklin, who had not long been out of jail. In 1912, Franklin had been a leading figure in the infamous Garrison Lane Vendetta between the Beach and Sheldon families and had been given ten years for shooting at Samuel Sheldon with intent to murder.

Kimber was obviously weakened by the loss of Franklin and his pals and by that of the other fourteen Birmingham hard men convicted after Epsom. He was now seriously threatened by the potent combination of the Sabinis, Solomon and his Jewish toughs, and also of Alf White and the King's Cross Gang. All three had been brought together by the cunning of Emanuel. It seemed that the reign of Billy Kimber as the most powerful gangster in England was drawing to an end. It was a false assumption to make. He fought back and fought back hard.

On July 5, 1921 there was a riot after Salisbury Races when Wal and Bert McDonald led the Elephant Boys in an attack on a gang of Solomon's men — whose leader, Jim Ford, was arrested by the police after they intervened to stop the fighting. About 50 men tried to rescue him and eventually seven other East Enders were arrested.

Then on August 18, The Times reported that the previous day "several bookmakers and their clerks were violently assaulted by gangs of roughs from Birmingham" at the Bath meeting. *The Guardian* agreed that the Birmingham betting men were the aggressors in this latest episode in the long-running vendetta between them and "a London gang of bookmakers and their protectors, who are mostly London Jews".

Estimated to be 200 strong, the Birmingham Gang also included Wal McDonald and some of his south Londoners. And as was to be expected with the highly intelligent Billy Kimber as their head, these men "had come to the city with a preconceived plan". Rumours of this had leaked out the night before and several London bookmakers and betting men returned to the capital the next morning. Amongst those who stayed was Alfie Solomon, who was especially hated by both the Brummagem Gang and the Elephant Boys as he was the man who had shot Kimber.

According to the *Daily Mail*, at about 10.30 in the morning Solomon and his clerk, Charles Bild, were walking to the races to set up their pitch. There are suggestions that Bild was actually Charles Solomon, 32 and perhaps the older of Alfie. In a widely syndicated article, including in the *Gloucester Citizen* of August 18, a special correspondent stated that as he left a shop, Bild was accosted by a man. Suddenly "a crowd of roughs closed round, and blows were rained on him from hammers, sticks, iron bars, and finally a sandbag". Covered with blood and almost senseless, Bild managed to escape and reached the Pump Rooms, where a maid tore up a sheet to bandage his wounds and whence he was taken to hospital by stretcher.

As for Solomon, he had been knocked out by a hammer. Four wounds were inflicted to his head and as he lay bleeding he was violently kicked and hit. His assailants then headed off and the injured man was taken to hospital. Gus Hall, a bookmaker from Brighton, and his clerk, Frank Heath, were subjected to similar outrages as they walked up Lansdown Hill. Described as a tall, powerful man aged 41, Heath was a friend of Solomon's and received a violent blow to the head which knocked him down.

He sustained severe scalp wounds, a fractured finger and cut knee, and just about able to pick himself up "he ran for dear life" downhill and was taken to hospital by a lorry driver. The *Daily Mail* added that Hall "was so badly knocked about that he was afraid to go the racecourse and asked the police to secure his property".

But as the *Dundee Courier* emphasised "these incidents were the preliminary to even more remarkable incidents". Gangs of "ruffians boarded three motor-coaches for the racecourse, and on the way were busy using field glasses for spotting victims". Near to St Stephen's Church, they made their drivers stop and swarmed out on the road "to set about a number of men who were walking to the races". One of the drivers noticed that on one of the seats there was "a formidable weapon, like a policeman's truncheon, lined with lead and studded with horse nails".

On the course itself there were ugly scenes. One man "piteously appealed to the police to be lifted over the rails" from the two shilling ring, where the Birmingham

Gang was rampant. He cried out in fear, "I shall be killed" and once he was taken outside by the police, "he ran like a March hare towards Bristol, never stopping to look behind him".

Immediately afterwards a force of between 200-300 men tried to rush the entrance to the ring, but were repulsed by the police. And as soon as racing was over, "several Italians sought police protection, and returned to London escorted by the police". It was also reported that one Italian from the capital had been attacked by a crowd of men and that he had drawn a revolver in defence. In fact he was not an Italian but was Harry Solomon, another brother of Alfie.

Three days after the Bath Races, the *Sunday Post* of Glasgow carried the headline on its front page: "Rival Bookies' Vendetta. Sequel to Wild Scenes at Racecourse". The story told of the appearance at court of Harry Solomon, charged with carrying a revolver and ammunition without a licence and with intent to endanger life. Looking ill, he appeared with a bandage around his head and was allowed to sit.

Police witnesses explained that whilst in the ring they saw a gang of men chase Solomon, who produced the revolver and directed it point blank at his pursuers. A short man ran at Solomon, knocked the revolver out of his hand and picked it up. Constable Stevens disarmed this man but then another person struck the accused. As he lay prostrate on the ground, Solomon was hit on the head with a hammer. The policeman then grabbed the aggressor but four or five other men from the crowd, which was estimated at between 100 and

150, bore him against the rails and forced him to release the man.

Solomon's defence lawyer, Mr Sharman, was concerned that two of the witnesses against his client came from Birmingham. *The Observer* of August 21 reported that attempts were made to solicit from them the identities of the assailants but "they denied any knowledge of the people taking part in the row". Mr Sharman stressed that his client was not the aggressor and that "he would have been killed if the police had not intervened".

He hoped that "justice would make other efforts to stop the terrible crimes occurring on racecourses". The chairman of the magistrates disagreed, declaring that the offence was a most serious one and sentenced Solomon to one month in jail. However like his brother, he had a violent reputation and was a particular target for the Birmingham Gang.

As for the two Birmingham witnesses, one was Charles Ansell from Somerset Street, off Cato Street in Duddeston. A toolmaker, he said that he had been terrified when Solomon drew his revolver and that after the arrest he had picked up a life preserver and razor that had been dropped on the ground.

The other witness from Birmingham was William "Cunny" Cunnington from Ladywood. Described as a dealer in oil polishing mops "he gave a stirring account of the chase of the accused, who, when the crowd pursued him made a leap for liberty over a paling, but tripped over an overcoat he was carrying". Billy Cunnington was a well-known betting man from

Ladywood and it is highly likely that if he were not one of the Birmingham Gang that he was friendly with its members.

It was obvious that Kimber was able to call upon very tough and frightening men from across Birmingham. One of them was Philip Thomas and he was charged with unlawfully wounding Solomon's clerk, Charles Bild. Born in 1896, he now gave his address as Unett Street in the Summer Lane neighbourhood. Ten years before, the 1911 Census recorded him as a polisher living with his parents and siblings in Tilton Road, which runs into Garrison Lane. However, like Kimber he seems to have been another prominent member of the Birmingham Gang who moved to London.

Brian McDonald writes that Thomas reinforces the connection between the Brummagem Boys and the Elephant Gang. In 1926 Thomas "was accused of being one of the Lambeth rioters, when a dispute between women of the Forty Elephants shoplifting gang caused a stir. His alibi that he had been in Birmingham at the time of the riot was supported by a policeman and he was acquitted. He later married Gert Scully, one of the girls who was gaoled for the riot." As their name suggested, the Forty Elephants were female thieves from the Elephant and Castle district of South London.

When Thomas came to court he was joined in the dock by Billy Kimber and William Joyce. Both were also charged with unlawful wounding and both gave their addresses as in London: Kimber in Islington and Joyce in Waterloo. Joyce's older brother, Edward, had been a betting man for a long time. In the 1911 Census he was living with his Irish-born parents in Allcock Street, Deritend and had given himself as a bookmaker. Four years before and aged 22, the *Gloucester Citizen* of October 28, 1907 had reported that he had been one of five young Birmingham men charged with not paying for their railway tickets on their way home from the Cheltenham Races.

By the early 1920s, Ted Joyce was another Birmingham racecourse man who had moved to London. As for the cases against his brother, Kimber and Thomas, they collapsed "in a curious way" as was noted in *The Guardian* on October 5, 1921. Strangely the prosecutor Bild was absent and nor was he represented by an advocate, whereupon the Chief Constable of Somerset said he had no further evidence to offer.

Defence counsel explained that his clients were prepared to submit to any court but observed "that there would be no more trouble of this kind". There had been a feud between certain sections of the race-going fraternity "but it had been amicably settled. Both public and police might rest assured that no breach of the peace would occur again". Thomas, Joyce and Kimber were then discharged. But the truce would be short-lived and more racecourse wars would break out before the end of the 1920s.

CHAPTER
SIX

Truces and Renewed Wars

The settlement between members of the "race-going fraternity" had arisen following more violence after the Battle of Bath. Two days afterwards, on Friday August 19, 1921, the Anglo-Italian and Jewish gangsters sought revenge at Hurst Park outside London. The *Dundee Courier* reported that a considerable number of "the boys" had turned up. They targeted a motor car owned by a Birmingham firm of bookmaker's that travelled all over the country. It looked like the vehicle was going to be demolished but fortunately the damage was small as the police were quickly on the spot. Mounted officers then "cleared the course at a gallop".

According to *The Times*, one man was arrested for carrying a hatchet. He was Aaron Jacobs, a 36-year-old bookmaker's clerk. The police explained that he had been accompanied by other men and as he passed through the turnstiles he declared, "if any of the — s are here today they will catch it". Described as a terror of the East End, Jacobs had a long list of convictions dating back to 1901. He was found guilty and sentenced to three months' hard labour. Three other men who had been carrying weapons had escaped the police.

110

Jacobs was a minder for a bookmaker called Alexander Crawford and despite the absence of the Birmingham Gang at Hurst Park, southern bookmakers remained fearful of what the *Glasgow Herald* called the "gangs of men who visited race meetings and terrorised bookmakers by any means which occurred to them". Consequently, on August 21, 1921, a number of them joined with some punters to form the Bookmakers and Backers Racecourse Protection Association. The chief movers were the bookmaker Walter Beresford and Edward Emanuel, who became the Association's president and vice-president respectively.

It seems that at this time, the Sabinis were under Emanuel's command, and he saw his involvement with the Association as an opportunity to finally and decisively wrest from Kimber control of the "services" given to bookies. Certainly, Emanuel became involved in printing the lists of runners for each race and he later set up a company which provided layers with tickets for their punters.

Emanuel moved quickly and within a month of the founding of the new Association, it appointed eight stewards at the high wage of £6 a week. Among them were Darby Sabini and Philip Emanuel, a relative of Edward Emanuel. Ron Whytock, a later secretary of the Southern Bookmakers Association, emphasised that "of necessity it was a question of fighting fire with fire in the early stages, and 'strong-arm' men were recruited to defend the members of the new Association".

Despite this, the new Association was welcomed by the Jockey Club, which ran many of the leading racecourses in England. Emanuel and the Sabinis benefitted from this legitimacy, which made it difficult for them to be challenged in the South by Kimber and the Birmingham Gang. Emanuel had made a shrewd and successful move in playing a prominent role in what would become the Bookmakers' Protection Association; however he had also hoped to take away from Kimber the racecourses in the west of England. He had failed, as the Battle of Bath had made plain.

With both sides at a stand-off and with the press demanding action from the police against the "hooliganism" and "ruffianism" on the turf, a meeting was called between the Birmingham Gang and the Sabinis. It arose after the Anglo-Italians sent out word that no Birmingham men should come south to make a book. In response, the Birmingham Gang warned that no southern bookmakers or their employees would be allowed to attend the September St Leger week at Doncaster.

Tom Divall, the former chief inspector at Scotland Yard who was employed by the racecourses to keep order at various meetings, stated that the Italians took up the challenge. They escorted Beresford, "the celebrated bookie", and his staff to King's Cross station: "the Italians, armed to the teeth, warned the enemy that, if they interfered in any way with that gentleman and his subordinates, they would slaughter the first man that placed a hand on them".

After searching the train they found no opponents; however when it arrived at Doncaster "it was met by an infuriated mob of the enemy". Some searched

Beresford and other London bookmakers "whilst others were hiding behind the iron pillars supporting the roof, behind taxis and in other places where they could be easily seen — all waiting to attack the Italians etc. They too were armed with razors and other murderous-looking weapons".

Finding none of their enemies, the Birmingham Gang ordered all of the London bookies back to the capital "and accompanied their commands with the most terrible threats". Beresford and his workers were allowed to remain and with "the whole 'Brum' gang then adjourned to the station refreshment room, and there took place the most awful and threatening conference in the history of racing".

It was agreed to follow this up with a meeting at Beresford's house, at which arrived "sixteen of both parties armed with revolvers and razors". Beresford himself called the Birmingham Gang "terrorists" in his speech at the inaugural banquet of the Bookmakers and Backers Racecourse Protection Association on December 6, 1921. Indeed he glossed over the meeting by explaining that "we met them here, and lengthily discussed the whole matter, and they promised there would be no more trouble". He implied that the Birmingham Gang had backed down. They had not.

In effect what happened was that they agreed to divide the country into spheres of control for the racecourse protection rackets. Those in the North, Midlands and West Country would be run by the Birmingham gangsters; those in the South and East Anglia by the Sabinis and their allies. The news of the truce made its way into the papers. On September 20, the *Nottingham Evening Post* reported that at the previous day's races in Leicester "the feud between the two London and Birmingham gangs had been settled, and there is no fear of any repetition of the undesirable proceedings which recently occurred in the south".

Ten days later, the *Western Gazette* observed that the two sides had gone on to meet at Newbury Races where it was authoritatively stated that "over a bottle they agreed to bury the hatchet". Then on October 5, the *Hull Daily Mail* carried the headline "Racecourse Feud. Is it a Settlement", following the collapse of the case against Kimber, Thomas and Joyce following the Battle of Bath.

In the negotiations, Billy Kimber and others had represented the hard men of Birmingham but behind the Sabinis were two powerful decision makers. They were Edward Emanuel, the guvnor of the Jewish underworld in the East End, who was moving into legal operations; and Walter Beresford, a leading southern racecourse bookmaker, who sought to push out "the low-class Birmingham men" as he declaimed them.

There was more than a hint of hypocrisy in Beresford's words as in 1902, he had been convicted as the proprietor of an illegal gaming house in London's West End and fined the huge sum of £200. Describing himself as a commission agent, a euphemism for an off-course bookmaker, he had also been convicted of running a house for betting on horses and had been fined another £50. A wealthy man from his unlawful activities, Beresford went on to become legitimate through his on-course bookmaking. It was he and Emanuel who were the promoters of the Bookmakers' and Backer's Protection Association, formed in late 1921 and which had gained the support of leading bookmakers in the London area as well as the Jockey Club. Indeed, Beresford stressed Emanuel's "very valuable assistance" in this move.

Emanuel and the Sabinis had not got as much as they had wanted from the truce but they did now control the highly-profitable south-eastern meetings along with those in East Anglia. Here their position was further strengthened by what appeared to be police collusion. Indeed in December 1922, the *New Statesmen* would allege that the Sabinis paid out £5,000 a year for its immunity from the police.

In these circumstances, Kimber had little choice but to agree to a truce — albeit one in which the Birmingham Gang retained control over the majority of England's racecourses. And as most of them still lived in Birmingham they were satisfied with their continued dominance of the rackets in the Midlands, North, South West and West Country. Unlike them, Kimber was very much London-based. He had been outwitted by Emanuel and Beresford and as a result his friends and allies in the capital had lost out.

The McDonalds and the Elephant Boys and George "Brummy" Sage and the Camden Town Mob were not prepared to take such a loss and a new racecourse war broke out in 1922 around the capital as Brian McDonald has detailed. Stabbings, razor slashings, shootings and even an attack with a machete on the

115

streets of London and at southern racecourses made the news.

During this violence, three letters were sent to the Home Secretary Edward Shortt in September and October 1922. They were postmarked Leicester and signed with the pseudonym "Tommy Atkins", the popular term given to British soldiers in general. As a former soldier and Englishman, the writer complained about the gangs of foreigners causing problems:

> The Financier and Brains of this gang of Cutthroats on the Race Courses of England are Foriengers named Edward Emanual and Gurchan Harris, these two men finance all the large clubs and Gambling Houses in the West End of London, and they pay large sums of money to other foriengers [sic], "The Sabini Gang" also the "Flying Squad" of Scotland Yard to safeguard their interests.

Gurchan Harris was most probably Gershon Harris, an associate of Emanuel and also from the Jewish East End.

The letters remain in Metropolitan Police files in the National Archives and the second, received on September 26, stressed the corruption of the police in their dealings with the Sabinis. They also documented attacks on members of the Birmingham Gang, including an assault on Andrew Towie at Epsom. A police investigation emphasised that there seemed to be little connection between this gang and the city "as, in fact, they were mostly convicted London thieves of the worst type". It is not surprising that this conclusion was reached given that apart from Kimber, Towie and a few others no Birmingham men were actually involved in the new racecourse war. Instead it was fought between London mobs.

In a fluid and ever-changing scene, there were also disputes between allies. The Sabinis quickly tired of Emanuel's control and they began to act in a manner which gave grave concern to the Bookmakers and Backers Racecourse Protection Association. On May 15, 1922, its Minutes recorded that an allegation was received that its stewards had demanded a royalty of a shilling on every set of lists that they sold. A month later, further complaints were dealt with and on September 4, the general committee of the Association agreed unanimously to dispense with the services of the stewards.

Then in November 1922 there was violent confrontation in London's Little Italy after the Sabinis fell out with their erstwhile friends the Cortesi brothers. These disturbances drew much attention from the newspapers. By contrast the Birmingham Gang continued their illegal activities but rarely attracted publicity. One mention came on September 7, 1922 when the *Derby Daily Telegraph* noted that John Gannon had been "charged with being a reputed thief and loitering in the second enclosure at the racecourse with the intent to commit a felony". Aged 32 and from Frankfort Street, Hockley, he had been accompanied by three others. A detective had watched them approach a bookmaker in single file, "without attempting to make any bets, and jostled the crowd". This was repeated later when Gannon "put his hand under a companion's coat and attempted to pick a pocket".

Gannon was supported by William Edward Thompson, a bookmaker from Edgbaston. He stated that he had employed the prisoner as his "tic tac" man for nine months and that he was honourable and honest and that he trusted him with large sums of money. A very different assessment was made by a detective from Birmingham who explained that Gannon had been convicted of theft and imprisoned in 1920. The prisoner then admitted to other crimes and was fined £10 or ten days in jail.

Other gangsters from Birmingham continued to intimidate bookies. On September 21, 1922 the *Western Morning News* reported that the Bookmakers' and Backers' Protection Association had prosecuted at Birmingham a Thomas Hawkins for demanding £2 from a bookmaker called Clowes, whilst he was waiting for a train to Stockton Races. Hawkins, a dealer, was accompanied by another man and when the money was not forthcoming "Clowes was severely maltreated". The Bench sentenced Hawkins to two months' imprisonment for the brutal assault.

In an interesting article on the on-going war between the London Gangs, the *Nottingham Evening Post* of September 23, 1924 pointed out that the "Hammer gang" from Birmingham "have been remarkably quiescent up to the present and so far have kept their word not to resort to violence in their tactics". The "good behaviour" of this "notorious Midland organisation" was because their leader, named as Ted Lewis, had pledged his word to confine "his adherents' depredations to the collection of tolls" from bookies at all northern meetings.

An instance of this leader's authority had come at Doncaster. A prominent racing man had been pickpocketed and buffeted and pushed by some of the local "boys". As soon as he could, the victim sought out the leader of the Birmingham Gang and within fifteen minutes his wallet and the £25 in it had been returned to him.

Ten months later, the newspaper had to print an apology to Edward "Ted" Lewis, "a well-known Birmingham commission agent", who "is a gentleman of the highest respectability" and who had no connection with the gang in question. It is not certain who the gang leader actually was, because it may not have been Billy Kimber.

By this time, it is probable that he had less influence in Birmingham as he had been established in London for over a decade and had now moved into the West End with the McDonald brothers. Their nephew Brian McDonald states that Kimber became a partner of "society nightclub queen Kate Meyrick, whose clubs attracted the early flapper society embarking on the Roaring Twenties". The way Brian's Aunt Ada told it was that Kimber protected her from bullies who tried to wring protection money from her. With these business interests, Kimber played a less important role in the new racecourse war that broke out in 1925 and which did involve the Birmingham Gang.

On June 16, the *Daily Mail* reported that seven men who were alleged to be race gang members had been charged with the severe wounding of Thomas MacDonald. He had been "found dazed outside a public house with severe razor slashes and head blows". Indeed, the prosecutor explained that his face was slit from ear to lip. One man was discharged but the others were said to have come to Birmingham to create a disturbance. In their defence, the men's solicitor declared that "MacDonald was a notorious fighter and bully among Midland race gangs".

Although he said that he was a caster from Hockley, MacDonald was a serious racing rough. Born in 1882, when he was just ten he had been given six strokes of the birch rod for the petty crime of stealing bread. Punished for being hungry, MacDonald went on to receive convictions for obstruction and gaming. Then in 1907 he was sentenced to nine month's hard labour for grievous bodily harm to a William Tooley. He was also handed six months to be served consecutively for assaulting a police officer.

Often operating under the alias of Thomas McDonough, MacDonald's scar was recalled by his stepson, Jackie Currigan — a member of a tough but fair Birmingham family which built up a big business of legal betting shops. Jackie told me that MacDonald was indeed a very hard man and that his razor scar did go from his ear to his lip.

According to some accounts the attackers were members of the Sabini Gang. If this were so then this was a new development, for none of the London gangs had previously dared to make any raids into Birmingham, even during the midst of the violent racecourse war of 1921. However it is unlikely as the Sabinis had already begun to wane in influence. Instead it seems that MacDonald's attackers were other Birmingham gangsters affiliated to the Birmingham Gang.

On June 23, 1925 the *Yorkshire Post and Leeds Intelligencer* informed its readers that four of the assailants were Moses Kimberley and Isaac Compston Kimberley, both of whom were agents; William Kimberley, a professional backer of horses; and Charles Kimberley, a bookmaker's clerk. All four were from Bordesley Green in Birmingham. The other two men were William Weston, a tailor, as was William Whitehouse from Camp Hill.

Two years previously, in a report in the *Evening Telegraph* on May 23, 1923, William Kimberley was given as a 31-year-old commission agent living in Paddington when he was charged with wounding Steve Griffin in a Camden Town pub. Detective Inspector Gillan gave evidence as to the violent character of Kimberley and his associates who were well-known as racing pests and who made their living from blackmailing bookies.

Griffin had been struck with a broken glass, giving him cuts to the throat and wrists. He was an associate of Alfie White and Alfie Solomon, both of whom were allied with the Sabinis. With two others they had previously beaten badly a bookmaker with a hammer and then pointed a revolver at him and kicked him. It seems, then, that Kimberley's attack was in revenge for this.

According to Brian McDonald, Kimberley had been born in Birmingham but was a member of George "Brummy" Sage's Camden Town Gang, which was allied to Kimber and the Birmingham Gang. Kimberley was indeed from Birmingham as was his family. In 1907, when he was a twenty-year-old cycle worker, he had been given eighteen months' hard labour at the General Quarter Sessions of the Peace in the Victoria Courts in the city. This was for breaking and entering a house with intent to steal.

His brother, Charles Kimberley, also had a bad record. Between 1907 and 1909, he was convicted for theft three times in Birmingham; whilst in 1910 he had been found guilty of shop breaking at Stafford. Then in September 1912 he was sentenced to three years in prison for breaking and entering a shop and stealing two costumes. At that time he was a hawker. The previous year, the 1911 Census showed the two brothers living with two other brothers, Isaac and Henry, and their parents in Allcock Street, Deritend. This was very close to the locations of the attacks in the Garrison Lane Vendetta.

MacDonald's slashing would suggest that there had been a serious fall-out within the always loose groups of villains that made up the Birmingham Gang and that the attack did not involve the Sabinis. As for the case of unlawful wounding against MacDonald, the prosecuting counsel took an unusual course. He stated that because the bandaged MacDonald admitted to being in a rival race gang he declined to give evidence. Consequently the case could not be continued and all the defendants were bound over to keep the peace for various sureties, bar for Charles Kimberley who was discharged.

MacDonald was then charged with "being a disturber of the peace and likely to persevere in such conduct". He promised not to attempt anything in Birmingham, though — to which statement the clerk of the court asked if he would get his own back elsewhere. MacDonald replied, "I have made up my mind, I don't care who knows it, to get my own back". The stipendiary advised him that he had better take care and told him not to be foolish. MacDonald was also bound over.

This assault on MacDonald came at a time when the *Western Daily Press* revealed that "disruptions had occurred" to the agreement between the Birmingham and London gangs to operate within different zones. The newspaper explained that this had been "scrapped, and the two separate and main gangs have been invading each other's preserves". This had led to a vendetta; whilst "peril and confusion" had been exacerbated by the emergence of new gangs.

It is likely that changes within the leadership of the Sabinis and also the Brummagem Boys was at the root of the new outbreak of war between them. Kimber's hold had lessened over the always loose gathering that was the Birmingham Gang. This had enabled the rise of men like MacDonald who were not prepared to adhere to agreements made with Kimber. Neither was Harry "Boy" Sabini, who was striving to assert his leadership of the Anglo-Italian gang and its allies, Solomon's Jewish gangsters and Alf White's King's Cross Mob.

In 1924, Harry's older brother, Darby was involved in a libel case against the *Topical Times*, which had declared that he led a gang of blackmailers. As a result, Darby had taken a back seat in the battles between the London gangs and Harry "Boy" had come to the fore. By then it seems that the power of the Sabinis had waned and Harry "Boy" was seeking to re-establish it. This decline in fortunes resulted from a number of factors, including the loss of Solomon, who was jailed for three years for manslaughter late in 1923.

By then the Sabinis had been dismissed as stewards by the Bookmakers' Protection Association and they had also suffered from their feud with the Cortesis. Brian McDonald also believes that Kimber and not the Sabinis remained in charge of the allocation of pitches at the highly-profitable meeting at Epsom. He did so through his longstanding friend, George "Brummy" Sage of the Camden Town Mob.

Harry "Boy" 's determination to reaffirm the Sabinis "rights" led him into conflict both with Sage's firm and the Birmingham Gang. In September 1923, the *Nottingham Evening Post* carried the headline "Sabini Boys Boys Busy Again". It was noted that they had recently broken the truce that had been in force since the beginning of the flat racing season in March.

Threatening letters had been sent to turf patrons and a number of frightened bookmakers had paid over money to them.

The next year, on July 15, 1925, the same newspaper stated that "open war has been declared between East and North London Gangs" and it was feared that attacks would be made on bookmakers. Just over a fortnight later, some of the Birmingham Gang razor slashed a rival. On the morning of July 30, 1925 a Birmingham commission agent called Sidney Payne was in the Embassy Club in Brighton. He returned to his hotel where he told his two friends that he had been insulted by a London bookie called Isaiah Elboz, originally from Whitechapel in the East End.

Payne's friends were William Glynn and Thomas Armstrong and they were also commission agents. In reality, though they belonged to "the Birmingham Boys", racing gang, according to the *Hull Daily Mail* of August 7. Armstrong was a particularly feared member who had been acquitted of killing Philip Jacobs, another East End Jewish bookmaker, in April 1921. Armstrong and Glynn returned to the Embassy with Payne where an eye witness said that as dancers were leaving the club he heard some men arguing: "blows were exchanged and there was turmoil. Someone drew a razor and there were screams followed by a free fight. There was great alarm in the street and all the available police in the district were rushed to the scene."

Just before they arrived a seriously injured man half-walked and was half-carried to a car. He was Elboz. Two other men, stewards at the club, were also badly injured. On August 6, the *Evening Telegraph* reported that the heavily-bandaged Elboz was loath to give evidence and was treated as a hostile witness. The prosecuting solicitor pronounced to the court that "you have to deal with a gang of very dangerous and violent men, who terrify people". Members of the Birmingham Boys, they had become reckless. Indeed, the prosecutor had never heard of "a more cold-blooded and ghastly attempt to maim and disfigure men from sheer spite". Granted bail, the three accused seem to have escaped further legal action.

James Cope was a villain and another leading figure in the Birmingham Gang. In 1906, when he was aged 25, he had received convictions for using obscene language, drunkenness and gaming; and a year later he was sentenced to three months' hard labour for breaking and entering into a shop and stealing money and goods. He gave his occupation as a polisher but in fact he was "a racecourse pest" and on April 30, 1924 the *Nottingham Evening Post* reported that he was charged with larceny for "welshing" at the Quorn Hunt Steeplechases.

PC Bramall had been on duty and had seen the prisoner dash between some coaches, pursued by some people who claimed that he had taken their bets and then run off with the money without paying those who had won. Cope denied that he was a bookmaker, even though he had on him betting tickets and an enamelled badge with the name of Jim Cope. Fortunately for him, the magistrates believed his story that he was "running", taking bets, for two other men who had disappeared.

Consequently, they sentenced him only to three months' hard labour.

James Cope had not been out of prison long when he and another man were prosecuted for unlawfully demanding money with menaces at Drayton Bassett. On December 27, 1924 the *Tamworth Herald* noted that the complainant from Erdington had also been assaulted but now said that "he did not want the Bench to take a serious view of the assault, and that he desired the charge of demanding money with menaces to be withdrawn".

Giving himself as a bookmaker from Stockton-on-Tees, Cope was bound over for £5 for the charge of assault and ordered to keep the peace for six months. His real identity was soon made plain in an event that made the *Manchester Guardian* on May 9, 1925 under the headline "Racecourse Gang at Chester". Seven men who "terrorised and blackmailed bookmakers" were rounded up after "an exciting conflict" in which a hammer was used and bottles were thrown.

Cope was described as their leader. He was sentenced to twelve months' hard labour for robbing a London bookmaker who "had fled in terror" from the gang. A Birmingham detective said that they were seldom brought to court because the bookmakers feared them.

Cope's conviction emphasised the determination of the police to stamp out the gangs that preyed on bookies and onlookers and which had become notorious again in 1925 with the flare up of the war between the Birmingham Gang and the Sabinis of London.

With cases like that of Cope, reports of ferocious affrays in London between racecourse gangs, a murder in the Sheffield Gang Wars, and the stabbing to death of an innocent Indian trader by a gang in Glasgow, it seemed as if gang violence was overwhelming urban Britain. And wherever it happened, there always seemed to be a connection to the race gangs — at least according to the press.

Under pressure, the Home Secretary, Sir William Joynson-Hicks, declared war against the racecourse gangs, as announced in the *Daily Mail* of August 27, 1925. He promised strong action and stiffer sentences. Despite this he went on to instruct the police to carry on as they had been doing. Yet because of the attention of the press and the authorities, the latest racecourse war was short-lived. Indeed on April 10, 1926 the *Exeter and Plymouth Gazette* revealed that the two "remarkable confederacies" had called a truce. They now held joint conferences "under a regular Chairman, at which they carefully allocate each other's respective spheres of activity, and settle plans and policy".

By now, though, the days of the racecourse gangs were numbered as was made plain in a report in the *Manchester Guardian* on May 1, 1928. Under the headline of "Race Gang Bully's Crimes" it recounted that Ernest Watts had been sentenced to five years for wounding. A man connected with the Elephant Boys, "Watts was a member of the gangs that assaulted bookmakers who declined to pay money when

128

blackmailed". Yet "since the gangs had been broken up he had inspired terror among inoffensive people".

That belief in the break-up of the gangs was a little premature, for as late as September 4, 1929 the *Derby Daily Telegraph* announced on its front page that a gang of nearly 25 pickpockets and cardsharpers from Birmingham had arrived for the races. They were dispersed by the police and their "movements were closely followed throughout the afternoon both on the course and in the chief rings" by plain clothes men.

Two months later, a short notice in the *Chelmsford Chronicle* on November 25 told of an attack on Benjamin Yeadon, and his son, Richard. Both were bookmakers and on July 16, they had been returning to London from Newmarket Races. With other racegoers, they stopped for tea at Sawbridgeworth where there was a quarrel with Philip Thomas and John Turner about a bet at a previous meeting at Lingfield. The two men assaulted the Yeadons, who had between £600 and £700 on them, and tried to rob them. The case against Thomas was discharged, whilst Turner pleaded guilty to common assault and was bound over to keep the peace.

Turner was 40 and a fish salesman from Shoreditch whilst Thomas was 33 and said he was a bookmaker. He was not; rather he was a nasty and violent member of the Birmingham Gang. He had been arrested for the attack on Bild in the "Battle of Bath" and was in the dock when Kimber and Joyce announced the first truce between the racecourse gangs. By now, however he was living in London and he gave his address as in Brixton, south of the Thames.

There seems to be more in the attack on Richard Yeadon than a dispute over a bet. He was the secretary of the Bookmakers Protection Association and, of course, that body was responsible for prosecutions against gang members and for helping clear the racecourse of protection racketeers. As a leading gang member and as someone who had benefited from such rackets, Thomas would have been aggrieved at Yeadon and other members of the BPA for curtailing their activities and incomes. Indeed the records of the Association state that Yeadon was attacked brutally and needed almost permanent police protection.

Fortunately, by now police action and arrests had contributed greatly to the decline of the racecourse gangs. So too did more severe sentences, and other factors such as the Home Secretary's instruction to the Flying Squad, the Specialist Crime and Operations section within the Metropolitan Police Service, to make racecourses safe. Led by the formidable Nutty Sharpe, the Squad targeted meetings where trouble was likely, and as Sam Dell put it, when he "walked on a racecourse they ran for their lives, every, all the villains ran".

His presence was appreciated also by the Jockey Club. Stung by the determination of layers to stamp out gangsterism, in 1924 this body had set up a department to supervise the rings. It engaged a number of inspectors whose duties were threefold: first, they were to watch the entrance gates and keep out undesirables; second, they were to patrol the rings to spy out welshers and known bad characters; and third, they were to look out for suspicious cases of disputed bets.

The senior supervisor of these men was a former soldier, W. Bebbington, and he made it clear in his book *Rogues Go Racing* (1947) that before the later 1920s, "the lot of a bookmaker was certainly a very unhappy one". However, by the end of that decade matters had improved enormously because of the combined action of the Jockey Club and the bookmakers' associations in the South, the Midlands and the North.

Their members advertised their honesty with badges which proclaimed their affiliation. They defended their integrity strenuously by prosecuting welshers who used their signs and by alerting the public to "mushroom bookies" — fraudsters who appeared at big meetings and who fled with their takings. Finally, the various BPAs formed Pitch Committees "to protect and safeguard racecourse bookmakers' rights". These could work only with the co-operation of the Jockey Club and from 1929 this was secured.

Henceforth pitches were not allocated by gangsters like Kimber or Sabini who took 50% from the winnings of the bookmakers who stood on them; instead they were allotted by Racecourse Personnel liaising with the local Bookmakers' Protection Association. When applying for a pitch a bookmaker had to have two established bookmakers willing to act as guarantors. The bookie's name was then added to a list and when a pitch became vacant it was passed according to the seniority of the layers on that list.

In one fell swoop, this system ended fights over pitches and it brought to an end the overseeing of the best of them by gangsters. By the later 1930s, in the Southern BPA's region, only two places remained where Pitch Rules could not be applied. These were the Downs at Epsom and Brighton; their exclusion was because neither area could be effectively enclosed. Consequently, there was some gang involvement at both meetings and it is not surprising that Graham Greene's novel of the underworld was set in the Sussex town.

The idea for *Brighton Rock* had come to Greene after he had read of an attack on a bookmaker and his clerk at nearby Lewes Races. As it was, this assault had nothing to do with pitches but with the death throes of the older gangs. Dodger Mullins had been slashed across the face by one of Alfie Solomon's men after a dispute at Great Yarmouth Races. In revenge, Mullins persuaded Jimmy Spinks of the Hoxton Mob and Wal McDonald of the Elephant Boys to join him in looking for Solomon at Lewes.

With over 40 gangsters tooled up, they found their quarry and badly beat him and his clerk. This attack prompted the *Daily Mirror* to proclaim "500 Gangsters Threaten New Race Track War". The alarmist headline vied with a previous announcement by the *Daily Express* that the racecourse gangs were "as well organised and nearly as ruthless as the racketeers of Chicago". Indeed, it seems apparent that in the

132

so-called race gangs, the media sought a comparison with the mobsters of the United States of America and in 1938 the *Daily Sketch* proclaimed, "The Gang Terror Here Now, Mobs Led by U.S. Criminals".

Greene avoided such hysteria. His characters were well drawn and not hyped-up examples of media fantasy. In a letter that he wrote to me in 1988 he explained that "my novel Brighton Rock it is true deals a little with something similar to the Sabini gang, but I have forgotten now what I may have known when I wrote it. In those days I used to go frequently to Brighton and once spent an evening with a member of a gang who introduced me to a certain amount of slang in use and took me to one of the meeting places of his fellow gangsters. But the details are beyond recall, and would be no good to you."

Two other factors inherent to the gangs were also crucial in their disappearance and have been overlooked. First, gang members were ageing; Jim Cope of the Birmingham Gang, for example, was in his early 40s when he was convicted. Second, was the loss of the two main leaders of the Sabinis and the Birmingham Gang. Darby Sabini and Billy Kimber had brought brains as well as brawn into their operations and that was missed. For two years from 1924, Sabini was preoccupied by an unsuccessful libel action against the publishers D.C. Thompson, an action that bankrupted him. He then moved to Brighton and set up as a bookmaker. As for Billy Kimber, the leader of the Birmingham Gang, he disappeared.

CHAPTER
SEVEN

Billy Kimber's New Life

In his intriguing and important book *Elephant Boys: Tales of London and Los Angeles Underworld* (Mainstream Publishing 2000), Brian McDonald relates how his uncles, the key hard men in the Elephant Boys of South London, were friends and allies of Kimber. One of them, Wag McDonald, fled to Canada to avoid arrest after the Battle of Epsom in 1921. Thence he moved to Los Angeles, where he became a bodyguard to Jack Dragna, the city's Mafia boss.

In about 1927, Wag's brother, Bert, and Billy Kimber also went to America after they had fired shots through the door of the Griffin, a drinking club used by the Sabinis. Through his Uncle Wag's Diary and the stories passed on by his Aunt Ada, Brian describes how Kimber went to Phoenix, Arizona where he may have killed a man who did not pay him the money owed for a favour. Chillingly, Kimber's oldest daughter from his first marriage, Maudie, used to say, "you owed our dad money, you paid with your life".

From Arizona, Kimber escaped to Los Angeles and then Chicago, where he was hidden by a friend from

England called Murray Humphreys — who was part of Al Capone's notorious gang. Thence he came back to England in about 1929. What then happened to Billy Kimber has been a mystery.

Charles Maskey worked for the big London bookie Billy Chandler and in 1988 he told me that Kimber became involved in Wimbledon Dog Track. Brian McDonald heard the same story, although his Aunt Ada believed that Kimber returned to Chicago and stayed there. In the event, he continued to operate on the racecourses of the south-west of England.

On March 23, 1925 the *Nottingham Evening Post* included a report on "a welshing incident" by Arthur Marshall, a Nottingham bookmaker, at the point to point meeting in Harwood, North Devon. Marshall had been surrounded by a hostile crowd after he left his pitch without paying out winning bets. As he was about to be arrested there was an interruption and he escaped. The policeman involved later saw Marshall, who had changed his bowler for a flat cap and his blue coat with a mackintosh.

As the offender was taken away by the officer, a bookmaker called Kimber declared that he would "offer a hundred pounds to a shilling that he is not the man". The accused was then surrounded by bookmakers' bullies who were protecting him from the angry crowd. Always an astute man, it seems that Kimber had realised that law and order was coming to the flat racecourses operated by the Jockey Club and to the jumps run by the National Hunt — but illegal money-making opportunities were still plentiful at

135

point to points. These were races for hunting horses and amateur riders over farmers' land — and significantly they were not well supervised.

Just over a year after this, on July 19, 1926 Kimber married Elizabeth Garnham at Holborn Register Office in London. He was now a widower aged 44 and she was 29. Kimber then went to America in 1927 and re-joined his wife when he returned to England two years later. However thereafter there is then no trace of him until March 1937 when the *Western Morning News* stated that he and his wife were amongst the many who had sent wreaths to the funeral of commission agent Joseph Cowell.

The next year, the same newspaper included several advertisements urging readers to "Bet with a reliable man Bill Kimber". He gave a Yeovil telephone number, whilst the advertisements related to his bookmaking at point to points across Devon and Cornwall. In October 1940, Kimber attended the funeral of another Devonian bookmaker and was noted as the president of the Devon and Cornwall Bookmakers' Association. There was a certain irony in that, as it was the founding of the BPA in 1922 that had sounded the death knell for his protection rackets on England's racecourses.

William Kimber died in 1945 at the Mount Stuart Nursing Home in Torquay. He was 63 and had suffered a prolonged illness. His obituary in the local newspaper asserted that "his great interest in life, both personal and professional, was racing and he was well known and respected on every racecourse in England".

His funeral was attended by many, but few would have known of his upbringing and past. One who was there and who did was his brother, Joseph. He had been in Billy's original gang of Birmingham pickpockets before 1914 and had received numerous convictions for frequenting and theft.

In 1943, two years before Kimber's death his arch-rival Edward Emanuel had died in Edmonton, North London — although the printing company that he set up continued for many years afterwards. Emanuel's ally, Darby Sabini, was interned during the Second World War under Defence Regulations because he was classed as a person of hostile origin. For all his many faults, that was an unfair accusation. Born in England of a British mother, his Italian father had died in 1902, he had never visited Italy and three of his brothers had fought in the First World War for Britain. Tragically, his only son, flight sergeant Ottavio Henry Sabini, was killed in Egypt in 1943 when his plane was shot down.

Later released from internment, Darby Sabini died in 1950 in Hove, when he was recorded as a commission agent. Harry "Boy" Sabini lived until 1978, whilst Alfie Solomon died in London in 1955. As for Andrew Towie, he carried on with selling dots and dashes in the Midlands and the North, although in 1940 the Northern Bookmakers' Protection Association made it clear that it was "entirely optional" to buy them and pay for number calling. It also pronounced that after Towie's death both operations would cease.

William Kimber left his widow the huge sum of £3,665. Born and raised in Birmingham's back streets, he died a rich man knowing that his daughters would lead a very different life to his own. Raised in a wealthy home they had privileged upbringings compared with the children by his first wife, Maude, who died in poverty in Birmingham in 1926 after he deserted her. His second daughter, Annie, had one child, Sheila, who has told her own daughter, Juliet Banyard, that:

they knew he had fled to America. Mom says they were under the impression he had had to leave, also that he had met and taken up with a wealthy woman he had met on one of the racetracks but actually he had ran off with her maid. He sent Annie a very expensive dressing table set, but they had to sell it as they were so poor. There must have been some contact with Annie as she knew he had come back to England and settled in Torquay. She also had a picture of him on the deck of a ship (with a woman).

Annie was informed of his death (Mom does not know who by) and on hearing of it said "Why should his new family get everything when there's us lot up here". She hired a solicitor to try and get some of his estate. Mom said he got Annie £1000. Maude, his oldest daughter, being illegitimate got nothing, but Annie split the money with her.

According to Mom, on receiving the money they set off for London and led the life of riley for a week. She remembers they all had new coats! Later they went on a holiday to Torquay to see where Billy had spent his final days. She thinks the address was Park Hill (it was) but they hadn't the nerve to knock the door.

A feared fighting man, powerful gangster, clever organiser of protection rackets and gangland alliances, and implacable foe to his enemies, Billy Kimber died a respected and legitimate businessman. His descendants, though, knew little about him. Juliet's brother, Justin Jones, emphasises this. Until he saw the Kemp brothers' *Gangs of Britain* episode on Birmingham on the Crime and Investigation Channel in 2013, "my family had thought of Billy Kimber as a criminal, we knew that much, who had done time in Winson Green. But we had absolutely no idea just what a major gangster he became. We had assumed he was simply a local thug. We are not particularly proud of his career, but of course it is rather exciting knowing one is directly related to a godfather of organised crime."

MY LIFE IN HOUSES

Margaret Forster

Margaret Forster takes us on a journey through the houses she's lived in: from the council house in Carlisle where she was born in 1938, to her beloved London house of today — via the Lake District, Oxford, Hampstead, and a spell in the Mediterranean. This is not a book about bricks and mortar, but a book about what houses are to us, and the effect they have on the way we live our lives. It takes a backwards glance at the changing nature of our accommodation: from blacking grates and outside privies to cities dominated by bedsits and lodgings; and houses today being converted back into single dwellings, all open-plan spaces and bringing the outside in. It is also a very personal inquiry into the meaning of home.

THE BUCKET

Allan Ahlberg

In 1938 Allan Ahlberg was picked up in London by his new adoptive mother and taken back to Oldbury in the Black Country. Now one of the most successful children's book writers in the world, here Allan writes of an oddly enchanted childhood lived out in an industrial town; of a tough and fiercely protective mother; of fearsome bacon slicers; of "fugitive memories, the ones that shimmer on the edges of things: trapdoors in the grass, Dad's dancing overalls". Of "two mothers, two fathers and me like a parcel or a baton (or a hot potato!) passed between them". Using a mix of prose and poetry, supported by new drawings by his daughter Jessica and old photographs, *The Bucket* brings to life the childhood that inspired Allan's classic picture books.